Gregg Herman

Settlement Negotiation Techniques in Family Law

A Guide to Improved Tactics and Resolution

Cover by Mary Anne Kulchawik/ABA Publishing.

The materials contained herein represent the opinions of the authors and editors, and should not be construed to be the views or opinions of the law firms or companies with whom such persons are in partnership with, associated with, or employed by, nor of the American Bar Association or the Family Law Section unless adopted pursuant to the bylaws of the Association.

Nothing contained in this book is to be considered as the rendering of legal advice for specific cases, and readers are responsible for obtaining such advice from their own legal counsel. This book is intended for educational and informational purposes only.

© 2013 American Bar Association. All rights reserved.

No part of this publication may be reproduced, stored in a retrieval system, or transmitted in any form or by any means, electronic, mechanical, photocopying, recording, or otherwise, without the prior written permission of the publisher. For permission, contact the ABA Copyrights and Contracts Department by e-mail at copyright@americanbar.org or fax at 312-988-6030, or complete the online request form at http://www.americanbar.org/utility/reprint.

Printed in the United States of America

18 17 16 15 14   6 5 4 3 2

Library of Congress Cataloging-in-Publication Data

Herman, Gregg M.
 Settlement negotiation techniques in family law / by Gregg Herman,
 Family Law, American Bar Association. — First Edition.
   pages cm
 Includes bibliographical references and index.
   ISBN 978-1-61438-898-2 (print : alk. paper)
   1. Divorce settlements—United States. 2. Compromise (Law)—United States. 3. Negotiation—United States. 4. Attorney and client I. American Bar Association. Section of Family Law. II. Title.
   KF535.H47 2013
   346.7301'5—dc23
                                                            2013003087

Discounts are available for books ordered in bulk. Special consideration is given to state bars, CLE programs, and other bar-related organizations. Inquire at Book Publishing, ABA Publishing, American Bar Association, 321 North Clark Street, Chicago, Illinois 60654-7598.

www.ShopABA.org

Contents

About the Author xi
Acknowledgments xiii

Introduction 1

Gandhi on Settlement 5

Chapter 1   *Getting to Yes*: Traditional Theory 7
    Optimal Method of Negotiation 8
    Four Principles of Principled Negotiation 8
    BATNAs 12
    Summary 13

Chapter 2   The Basics 15
    When to Negotiate 15
    How to Negotiate 17
    Making the First Offer 19
    Simplifying the Process 20
    Order of Negotiation 20
    Big Picture Versus Little Picture 21
    Summary 22

Chapter 3 Timing 23
Stages of Divorce Proceedings 23
Importance of Timing 24
Timing Issues... 25
Recognition of the Right Time 26
Summary.. 27

Chapter 4 Controlling Emotions 29
Emotions: The Positives and the Negatives 30
Dealing with Emotions 30
Summary.. 34

Chapter 5 Preparing the Client for Settlement 35
Convincing a Client to Negotiate... 35
Preparing Yourself... 37
The Client Meeting 38
The Meeting Agenda... 38
Establishing Reasonable Goals... 40
Summary.. 40

Chapter 6 Disclosure.. 41
Benefits of Full Voluntary Disclosure...................................... 41
Methods of Providing Disclosure 43
Summary.. 44

Chapter 7 Positional Negotiation.. 45
Advantages 45
Three Positions 45
Ultimatum Versus Compromise 48
Summary.. 50

Chapter 8 Negotiating with Opposing Counsel 51

The "Book" on Opposing Counsel 51

Establishing Rapport with Opposing Counsel 52

The Intimidating Negotiator 52

The Unethical or Untrustworthy Negotiator 53

The Cooperative versus Competitive Negotiator 54

The Best Friend as Opposing Counsel 54

Summary 56

Chapter 9 Negotiating with the Pro Se Party 57

Negotiation Strategies 57

Risks in Negotiating with Attorney Se 60

Summary 61

Chapter 10 The Four-Way Meeting 63

When to Meet and When Not to Meet 64

Whose Office? 64

Preparing for the Meeting 65

The Meeting 66

Concluding the Meeting 67

Summary 67

Chapter 11 The Role of the Judge 69

Facilitating Settlement 70

Conducting Pretrials 72

Meeting with Clients 72

Understanding Practicalities 73

Summary 73

Chapter 12   Planned Early Negotiation ... 75
- Prison of Fear ... 76
- PEN: Positives and Negatives ... 78
- Summary ... 79

Chapter 13   Family Law–Specific Settlement Issues ... 81
- Children ... 81
- Support ... 85
- Summary ... 87

Chapter 14   Mediation ... 89
- Reasons for the Success of Mediation ... 89
- Pitfalls of Mediation ... 90
- Selection of a Mediator ... 92
- Preparation for Mediation ... 93
- Postsettlement ... 94
- Summary ... 94

Chapter 15   Collaborative Divorce ... 95
- Agreement to Proceed ... 97
- The Disqualification Agreement ... 98
- The Role of the Mental Health Professional ... 98
- The Role of the Financial Professional ... 98
- The Role of the Judge ... 99
- Downsides of Collaborative Divorce ... 99
- Summary ... 102

Chapter 16   Cooperative Divorce ... 103
- Collaborative Divorce: An Overview ... 103
- Cooperative Divorce: An Overview ... 104

    The Role of the Mental Health Professional 106
    The Role of the Financial Professional 106
    The Role of the Judge 107
    Why Bother with a Cooperative Agreement? 107
    Summary 108
    Sample Form: Cooperative Divorce Agreement 109

Chapter 17 Creative Settlement Techniques 111
    Cut the Cookie 111
    The Buy-Sell Offer 112
    The Nontrial Trial 113
    The Joint Recommendation 114
    Phone a Friend 115
    The Curse of Too Much Money 116
    Taking an Issue off the Table 116
    Acts of Loving Kindness 118
    Summary 118

Chapter 18 Divorce Settlements and Game Theory 121
    Game Theory Background 121
    The "Game" of Divorce 122
    Utilization of Game Theory in Divorce 127
    Summary 128

Chapter 19 Ethical Considerations 129
    Truthfulness 130
    Withdrawal 131
    Collaborative Law 134
    Respect for the Opposing Side 135

Communication with Clients 136

Improper Mixing.. 137

Summary... 137

Chapter 20 Ten Commandments 139

Rule One: Be Cordial 140

Rule Two: Do Not Give Ultimatums 141

Rule Three: Do Not Give Deadlines 141

Rule Four: Make Full Disclosure Voluntarily and Freely 142

Rule Five: Don't Be Afraid of Taking the First Step 143

Rule Six: Never Negotiate Backward 144

Rule Seven: Never Refuse to Negotiate 145

Rule Eight: Never Get Personal 146

Rule Nine: Never Get Angry at a Settlement Proposal 147

Rule Ten: Be Prepared!... 147

Summary... 148

Chapter 21 The Endgame 149

The Client Knows Best... 149

Footsteps and Last-Minute Agreements 150

Judicial Roadblock 150

Minting Negotiable Currency 151

Money to Warm Cold Feet.. 151

A Few Strains of "Kumbaya"... 152

Summary... 153

Chapter 22 Becoming a Better Negotiator 155

Read This Book 156

Read Other Material 156

Watch Other Lawyers 157

Take Courses in Negotiating 158

Take Courses in Related Skills 158

Be Self-Critical 159

Get Feedback from Other Attorneys 159

Get Feedback from Former Clients 160

Be Creative 160

Summary.. 161

Index.. **163**

About the Author

Gregg Herman is a shareholder with the law firm of Loeb & Herman, S.C., which practices exclusively family law, concentrating in cases with significant assets or income. He is a 1974 graduate of the University of Wisconsin and 1977 graduate of the University of Wisconsin law school.

From 1977–1984, Gregg was an Assistant District Attorney for Milwaukee County, prosecuting nearly 100 jury trials ranging from white-collar crime to First Degree Murder. He joined Leonard Loeb in the practice of family law in October, 1984.

Gregg is a Fellow of the American Academy of Matrimonial Lawyers and is on its Board of Governors (2012–2015). He is Board Certified in Family Law Trial Advocacy by the National Board of Trail Advocacy. He is the Court Commissioner for Branch 46 of the Milwaukee County Circuit Courts, serving the Hon. Bonnie Gordon.

Gregg was chair of the American Bar Association Family Law Section from August 2007 through August 2008. He was also the Founder of the Cooperative Divorce Institute, Inc. and served as its first chair from 2003–2005 and the founder of the Collaborative Family Law Council of Wisconsin, Inc. and its first State-wide Chair from 2000–2001.

Gregg Herman is co-author of *The System Book for Family Law* published by the State Bar of Wisconsin and is a contributing editor to the *American Journal of Family Law*. He was Editor-in-Chief of the *Wisconsin Journal of Family Law* from 2002 to 2004 and has been the editor of three editions of *101+ Practical Solutions for the Family Lawyer* and *The Joy of Settlement*, both published by the ABA Family Law Section.

Gregg received the "Leader in the Law" award by the *Wisconsin Law Journal* in 2007 and was the recipient of the 2003 Chairs award from the ABA Family Law Section for "meritorious service exceeding what is expected of our leadership."

Gregg is a former President of the Milwaukee Bar Association (1998–1999), the Wisconsin chapter of the American Academy of Matrimonial Lawyers (1999), and is a past chair of the State Bar of Wisconsin Family Law Section (1996–1997). He is formerly a member of the Board of Governors of the State Bar of Wisconsin (1999–2003, 2004–2006), and a member of Council of the ABA Family Law Section (1996–2003).

In his personal life, Gregg's passions are his family (his wife of 32 years, Susan, three children, and one grandchild), the Wisconsin Badgers, and his Labrador retriever—not necessarily in that order!

Acknowledgments

The starting point for this book was the many wonderful chapter contributions from the various authors of *The Joy of Settlement*, which I edited.[1] Although I quoted from many of these chapter authors, I drew inspiration from far more; and to the extent that this book has any useful suggestions or ideas, credit goes to those authors whose work is the foundation on which such suggestions and ideas are built.

Early in this project, I engaged paralegal Lucy Kelly and newly minted lawyer Rochelle Johnson. Both helped to provide the original research that guided me in writing this book.

Several lawyers, including Richard Podell, Charles Phillips, and Randy Kessler, shared experiences, stories, and ideas, all of which were valuable.

My associate, Kelley Shock, assisted with proofreading; and my other support staff, Belinda Lathan and Regina Williams, were also of assistance.

My contact with the editorial board, Joe Booth, gave me some ideas and direction but, most important, periodically checked on my progress to make sure that the book would be completed on time. Just knowing that I would get an e-mail from Joe prompted me to get to work!

My thanks to the entire Publications Board of the American Bar Association (ABA) Family Law Section, so ably chaired by Gail Baker, for having confidence in me. Having served as a member of the board for seven years, I know how difficult its work is—and having served as an officer of the section, I also know valuable it is.

Thanks are specially due to Sheila Sybrant, who served as my professional editor. It is amazing how different—and better—this book reads after she was done editing it. She is a true professional and it was a pleasure working with her.

---

1. AM. BAR ASS'N, THE JOY OF SETTLEMENT (Gregg M. Herman ed., 1997).

Finally, my thanks to all of the lawyers out there whose goal, as professionals, is to help their clients by working hard to resolve cases through settlement.

Introduction

In 1995, I was asked to assume a project that had been languishing for some time: editing a compilation of articles about divorce settlement negotiations for a book. With the assistance of a number of fine family law attorneys, I was able to complete the project, and the result was *The Joy of Settlement*, published in 1997 by the ABA Family Law Section (FLS).[1] *The Joy of Settlement* sold a respectable number of copies, but, a few years later, the ABA FLS published a book on litigating divorce cases. It outsold *The Joy of Settlement* several times over.

Over the years, I have had the privilege to speak about various aspects of divorce settlement negotiations before a number of bar associations, including the Kentucky Bar Association, the Alaska Bar Association, and the Association of Family and Conciliation Courts, to name a few. On each occasion, I have asked for a show of hands to determine the percentage of cases settled, rather than litigated, by the lawyers in attendance. I start with 75 percent, and every single hand in the room is up. In fact, hands don't even start going down until I get to 85 percent. Most

---

1. AM. BAR ASS'N, THE JOY OF SETTLEMENT (Gregg M. Herman ed., 1997).

hands are still up at 90 percent, a fair number at 95 percent, and even some at 100 percent. Although unscientific to be sure, this survey reflects what I've always believed: most lawyers prefer to resolve—rather than litigate—cases.

The problem is that most legal education, both in writing and through lectures, teaches what lawyers engage in the small minority of the time: litigation. The fault is not with the publishers or legal education providers; rather, the fault lies with lawyers, who think that they need training for litigation but not for settlement. The irony of this belief is starkly highlighted in visits to bookstores, which contain large numbers of books on negotiations, and in perusals of college business school course listings. In business settings other than law, there is a widespread understanding of the importance of learning how to negotiate. The Harvard Business School course on negotiation is sold out far in advance, for example. Still, lawyers seem to believe that settlement is intuitive and therefore does not require the same training as litigation.

To be sure, to an extent, negotiation strategy can be intuitive. But not all negotiation strategy is instinctive. Therefore, family law attorneys should use the substantial amount of literature and courses teaching the strategy and concepts to become better negotiators.

The importance of becoming better negotiators cannot be understated. What we do affects not only the lives of our clients but also the lives of their children and their extended family. Although it's important to get to "yes" so that our clients can avoid the financial and emotional destructive nature of litigation, if we can get to "yes" with less acrimony and bitterness, we have done a great service for our clients. My late partner, Leonard Loeb, used to say that the goal of a family law attorney should be to resolve a case without creating or adding to the degree of animosity that would prevent parents from walking down the aisle together at their child's marriage. Importantly, that methodology is not inconsistent with also achieving superior financial results for our clients. In fact, it is quite consistent.

Consider the typical case of an income provider who is going to pay support. Many wage earners have a certain amount of discretion regarding the creation of income. In extreme cases, some simply quit their jobs, running the risk of being sanctioned for contempt. More commonly, they have options regarding how hard to work and how much to earn. If the wage earner has any control over his business, there are numerous methodologies (some of them quite legal) to minimize his income for the purpose of support while taking benefits in other forms (sometimes not quite so legal). Working voluntary overtime or second jobs or even changing jobs are other ways of creating extra income—or not. A good relationship between the parties can lead to a higher incentive to work and create wealth, from which all will benefit.

There are many schools of thought about negotiations, including some lawyers who believe that litigation is as acceptable as settlement. Litigation allows some lawyers to pass the blame for less-than-optimal results, which are endemic in settlement because settlement requires compromise. Others believe that courts can do as good a job in making any compromises as the parties can themselves. Still others believe that settlement is not part of being a lawyer, i.e., that lawyers, in the words of the now-repealed *Model Code of Professional Responsibility*, "zealously" advocate for their clients.[2] This book is not for those lawyers unless those lawyers want to explore changing their minds. Rather, it is written under the belief that by recommending compromise to clients and taking full responsibility for recommending what trade offs should be made, lawyers are doing exactly what they should be doing: helping clients end one part of their lives and have an opportunity for a better future. Zealously advocating for a client does not accomplish any of the foregoing and is therefore, in my opinion, completely inconsistent with an attorney's responsibilities.

This book is not designed for the novice family law attorney, nor is it a PhD course in settlement negotiations. Although it's designed for those lawyers who have done enough negotiating to recognize room for improvement, it is not intended to replace—or even summarize—the vast collection of resources for learning the science of negotiating. Instead, it is designed to collate, using one voice, many of the various concepts of divorce settlement negotiations that are discussed in *The Joy of Settlement*, for which I owe the authors a deep debt of gratitude. Hopefully, having waded into the water with these concepts, lawyers will go the next step and dive in the deep end for further information and to improve their skills.

It will be noted that in the course of writing this book, I frequently use pronouns assuming that the female member of the couple will be the primary child custodian and the male, the primary financial provider. I well recognize that such assumptions are inconsistent with

---

2. MODEL CODE OF PROF'L RESPONSIBILITY Canon 7 (1980).

many couples in today's world, but attempting to use neutral or mixed terms (e.g., *his/her*) does not seem to read well, so the common, but certainly not universal, gender role assignments are assumed for the most part.

There is an old joke that 80 percent of lawyers give the other 20 percent a bad name. This is a joke because the truth is that the vast majority of lawyers are highly professional. Like all professionals, their goal is not to line their own pockets but to provide services to promote the best interests of their clients. Far more than 80 percent of lawyers deeply understand that settlement promotes those interests. I hope that this book is of some assistance to them.

Gandhi on Settlement

My joy was boundless. I had learnt the true practice of law. I had learnt to find out the better side of human nature and to enter men's hearts. I realized that the true function of a lawyer was to unite parties riven asunder. The lesson was so indelibly burnt into me that a large part of my time during the next twenty years of my practice as a lawyer was occupied in bringing about private compromises of hundreds of cases. I lost nothing thereby—not even money, certainly not my soul.

—Mohandas K. Gandhi, An Autobiography: The Story of My Experiments with the Truth (1957)

Getting to Yes: Traditional Theory

Any book on settlement negotiations must acknowledge the seminal work on negotiations, *Getting to YES: Negotiating Agreement Without Giving In* by Roger Fisher and William Ury.[1] In this book, the authors propounded "principled negotiation," a method of negotiation emphasizing that the focus in negotiation should not be simply winning but rather developing an agreement that is wise, fair, and long-lasting and—most important—will satisfy the interests of both sides and the larger community (friends, family, children) surrounding the two parties.[2] The four principles comprising this method have applicability to divorce settlement negotiations.

---

1. ROGER FISHER & WILLIAM URY, GETTING TO YES: NEGOTIATING AGREEMENT WITHOUT GIVING IN (1981).
2. *Id.* Principled negotiation was developed by the Harvard Negotiation Project; it is also called "negotiation on the merits." *Id.* at 10.

Optimal Method of Negotiation

According to Fisher and Ury, "any method of negotiation may be fairly judged by three criteria: It should produce a wise agreement if agreement is possible. It should be efficient. It should improve or at least not damage the relationship between the parties."[3] Under these criteria, "[a] wise agreement can be defined as one which meets the legitimate interests of each side to the extent possible, resolves conflicting interests fairly, is durable, and takes community interests into account."[4]

In many situations, negotiations will take the form of positional bargaining. In a positional bargaining situation, the parties begin by stating/defining their position on a particular issue. After that has been done, the parties begin to bargain from their opening position with the goal of moving closer to the center and an eventual agreement (see chapter 7, "Positional Negotiation"). Fisher and Ury argued that positional bargaining can be an inefficient means of negotiating. The agreements that are reached do not necessarily protect the interests of both parties but rather can cause the parties to become stubborn and damage their future relationship.[5] Therefore, Fisher and Ury advanced the use of principled negotiation.

Four Principles of Principled Negotiation

In principled negotiation, there are four principles: "[s]eparate the people from the problem"; "[f]ocus on interests, not positions"; "invent options for mutual gain"; and "[i]nsist on using objective criteria."[6]

Separate the People from the Problem

The first principle is to separate the people from the problem. This means separating "people problems" from any substantive issues (bargaining points) and dealing with them separately and outside of the negotiations.[7] People problems are any problems that arise from

---

3. *Id.* at 4.
4. *Id.*
5. *Id.* at 6.
6. *Id.* at 10–11.
7. *Id.*

"perception, emotion, and communication,"[8] which in family law frequently overshadow the substantive issues involved.

As every divorce lawyer well knows, getting past people problems is not that easy. After all, it is people problems that led to the parties divorcing in the first place. Clients do not come from a vacuum: they come from a history that typically includes at best poor communication and cooperation at best and a history of mistrust, sometimes for good cause, at worst. These factors continue when lawyers and the legal process get involved. It is critical that family lawyers try to recognize these emotions. Many times, it is necessary to afford one or both sides an opportunity to release some steam in order to reach the substantive issues. In these cases, lawyers should not react to the parties' emotional outbursts.

Fisher and Ury noted that communication problems are people problems as well.[9] The parties in a divorce may not be talking to each other but rather are talking to another audience, perhaps "playing to the crowd," hoping to get a response. Therefore, instead of listening to the other side, they are planning a response. It is crucial to the negotiations that both parties begin to listen actively and acknowledge what the other party is saying. After all, if no one is listening, what's the point in talking?

Failing to listen is a fault not just of the clients but of lawyers as well. An experienced colleague once told me that the most important attribute for a successful negotiator is the ability to listen. However, law school does not teach listening. Law school teaches advocacy and issue resolution, both of which are active skills; listening is a passive skill.

Some years ago, I had the opportunity to sit in on some mediation sessions conducted by a brother-sister team of social workers, Mimi and Chic Nichol. My role was guardian ad litem for the children, which in Wisconsin is a lawyer appointed for the children's best interests. I was asked to sit in on mediation sessions, with the consent of both parties, but not to participate unless I was directly asked. Being forced to listen and not talk was a new experience. I realized how many times Mimi and Chic, trained as social workers, would pick up on something said by a party that I would have missed if I was planning a response. As lawyers, our training is primarily to advocate, which is an active skill.

---

8. *Id.*
9. *Id.* at 22.

By developing the passive skill of simply listening, we can become far better negotiators.

Focus on Interests, Not Positions

The second principle is to negotiate about interests, not positions—things that you really want and that you really need.[10] In many cases, these two things are often not the same. Again, this is especially true in divorce negotiations. One common example is the client whose position is to inflict damage on the other party. Another common example is the client who negotiates less about what she gets and more about what the spouse does *not* get. For better or worse, getting a client to recognize her true interests and to negotiate for them constitutes one of the chief people problems discussed earlier.

Invent Options for Mutual Gain

When the parties involved begin to focus on their interests, it becomes easy to get to the third principle: inventing options for mutual gain. This means that the negotiating parties should begin to look for solutions that will allow both sides to win and not just continue to fight from the original position, i.e., one side must win and the other side must lose.[11] Again, the application to divorce negotiations is present here. In a support case, for example, the typical final result of negotiations is for the payer to feel that he paid too much and the recipient to feel that she did not receive enough. Yet, it benefits the payee if the payer feels that he "won," whatever that means in the particular context. After all, a payer who feels that the settlement is not beneficial has no incentive to make the agreement work. Payments may be late or missed if the payer has any control; and if the payer has no control, the payer has an incentive to try to modify the payments as soon as possible to remedy the perceived injustice.

The key to this principle is to "generate a variety of possibilities before deciding" on a course of action in order to "respond to the difficulty of designing optimal solutions while under pressure."[12] Fisher and Ury suggested that such pressure constraints can be alleviated by "setting aside a designated time within which to think up a wide range

---

10. *Id.* at 40.
11. *Id.* at 57.
12. *Id.* at 10–11.

of possible solutions that advance shared interests and creatively reconcile differing interests."[13] As all lawyers know, some cases can only be settled on the courthouse steps (sometimes literally). It is in those instances that advance preparation is essential. In criminal cases, it's called the "footsteps of the jury" syndrome: the imminence of trial suddenly makes a plea bargain begin to sound more appealing. Planning for such a possibility before getting to court and discussing it with the client is of critical importance.

A divorce lawyer should never assume that there is one "fixed pie" with only one way to divide it; it is necessary to "[i]dentify shared interests" so that either the pie can be made larger or it can be divided in a way that both sides get the piece they want.[14] In order to do so, it is necessary to take the other side's needs into account when making a proposal. It takes no skill whatsoever to ask for everything—and it will take no skill whatsoever for the other side to simply reject the proposal. The skill in negotiating is to make a proposal that causes the other side, at a minimum, to make a counterproposal. Therefore, when making a proposal, the lawyer must place himself in the shoes of the opposing counsel and imagine what response is likely.

Insist on Using Objective Criteria

The fourth principle is to always insist on using objective criteria when making decisions.[15] If some outside, objective criteria can be found, it can make the negotiation process a lot simpler. For example, in labor negotiations, management and union representatives will look at what similar businesses and unions have agreed to. This will give both sides more information on what is fair, and it makes it a little harder to oppose offers.

The application to legal proceedings, including family court cases, is obvious. The objective criterion is what a court would likely do at the conclusion of a contested trial. After all, if the parties knew the eventual results, they might as well just agree and avoid the costs of trial. This is why evaluative mediation is often so successful. (Later in this book [see chapter 17, "Creative Settlement Techniques"], I will discuss the "nontrial trial," which is another means of determining the

---

13. *Id.*
14. *Id.* at 70.
15. *Id.* at 81.

objective criterion.) This is also why the best negotiators have at least a certain amount of trial experience. Yes, there are excellent negotiators who have never tried a case, and negotiators can learn what courts are likely to do by talking to judges and other lawyers. But experience is the greatest teacher, and being able to share from personal experience such objective criteria with a client—or with the opposing counsel—makes a lawyer a better negotiator.

BATNAs

Negotiators need to know the best alternatives in order to optimize principled negotiation. Fisher and Ury created the concept of and strongly suggest the development of a "BATNA," an acronym for Best Alternative To a Negotiated Agreement.[16] Brad Spangler, in an article about BATNAs, wrote that BATNAs are important to negotiations because a person cannot decide whether to accept a proposed agreement without knowing the available alternatives.[17] A BATNA, according to Fisher and Ury, can protect a person from accepting something that is not favorable and from rejecting something that is favorable.[18] As summarized by Spangler, "if the proposed agreement is better than your BATNA, then you should accept it. If [it] is not better," then you should either continue negotiating or prepare for trial.[19]

In the process of figuring out a BATNA—which can be developed "for any negotiation situation," from a "simple task" to a "complex problem"—a person should "consider the alternatives available to the other side."[20] People tend to become "overly optimistic about . . . their options. . . . The more you can learn about [your opponent's] options, the better prepared you will be for negotiations."[21]

Perceptions and realities impact the success of BATNAs in negotiations, according to Spangler. If the parties have different views or

---

16. *Id.* at 97.
17. Brad Spangler, *Best Alternative to a Negotiated Agreement (BATNA)*, BEYOND INTRACTABILITY (June 2012), http://www.beyondintractability.org/bi-essay/batna.
18. FISHER & URY, *supra* note 1, at 103.
19. Spangler, *supra* note 17.
20. *Id.*
21. *Id.*

"dissimilar images" about the BATNAs, there could be a hold in the negotiations or even a retraction of an offer.[22] And, added Spangler,

> *If both sides' BATNAs tell them they can pursue the conflict [in court] and win, the likely result is a power contest. If one side's BATNA is indeed much better than the other's, the side with the better BATNA is likely to prevail. If the BATNAs are about equal, however, the parties may reach a stalemate.*[23]

Summary

These concepts, and many more advanced ones, form a core of negotiating theory that extends far beyond the scope of this book. As suggested in chapter 22, "Becoming a Better Negotiator," doing further research and learning advanced theory can only be beneficial to the divorce negotiator, as it would be to any negotiator. For the limited scope of this book, however, we pay homage to the seminal work of Fisher and Ury and attempt to apply their theories to the field of divorce law.

---

22. *Id.*
23. *Id.*

The Basics 2

Some basic concepts and suggestions warrant discussion at the outset. Of course, nothing is "one size fits all," so for each suggestion, you should do what fits the individual circumstances of each case and the contours of your personality and style.

When to Negotiate

There is only one hard-and-fast rule regarding when to negotiate: never, ever, ever go to trial without making an attempt to negotiate, no matter how useless such an effort may seem.

In a perfect world, negotiations wouldn't start until both sides have completed full discovery. In the real world, due to the importance of settlement and the financial limitations of the parties, it is frequently necessary to start negotiations without enough information to make the process meaningful, but with confirmation information to follow. The process is somewhat similar to making bets in stud poker: you are betting on the cards that have been dealt that you can see and basing future action on upcoming information.

At the very least, however, you should not start without a signed financial disclosure statement from the other side. Absent such, it would be easy for the other side to manipulate the process by changing the information that serves as its basis.

Where there are hearings during the course of a case, either for a pendente lite or other interim orders, an optimal time to negotiate may be when you have a favorable result. Too many lawyers soak in a victory rather than recognizing that negotiating from a position of strength is an advantage. Conversely, if the hearing did not go well for your client, it is usually preferable to avoid final negotiations until matters improve—if you think that they might.

There is a school of thought that counsels against negotiating on the day of trial. The reasoning, which has a great deal of validity, is that the pressure on counsel and clients is too immense and mistakes are too easy to make. I am not a proponent of that school of thought. To some extent, you can ameliorate the pressure by preparing your client (and yourself) for last-minute negotiations. Negotiations by ambush is not a preferable means of settlement, but if you have identified your bottom line ahead of time, getting there under pressure is still better than not getting there at all.

The start of a trial does not have to end negotiations. Again, not all lawyers agree with me on this point, but two things can happen—and usually do—during a trial that can make negotiations fruitful. One is that your case is going better than anticipated. As stated earlier, you are always better off negotiating from a point of strength. The other is that your case is going worse than anticipated. Obviously, this is not ideal, but it may be a wake-up call that you need to reassess the perceived strength of your case. As a colleague of mine put it, "[l]awyers need to check their ego at the door and do what's best for their client." Sometimes that may mean going hat in hand to opposing counsel after a bad start at trial.

And the trial court's decisions do not end after a trial. Some of the best settlements I have negotiated have been *after* a trial, sometimes even while the case was on appeal. There is a good reason for this: after a trial, both sides have the objectivity of knowing what a particular court would do. Sometimes that can aid the settlement process. A good example is a support buyout. If you know what a judge *would* order because he has already made the order, the buyout number is apparent to both sides. Therefore, negotiations can take place in light of the litigation alternative.

And, no, during appeal is not the final time to settle a case. Sometimes emotions are so raw during a divorce and immediately afterward that interest-based negotiations are not possible. A very angry woman I represented once would not agree to any reasonable settlement before, during, or immediately after her trial. Years later, when the case came back for modification of support, I asked her if she was ready to settle. She was and the case settled.

The short and simple basic concept: settlement can happen at any time. Never let your ego preclude consideration of settlement no matter where you are in the divorce process.

How to Negotiate

It seems a generality in this chapter: there should be no hard-and-fast rules for the basics of negotiation (other than, of course, ethics and civility). So, although there are many ways to negotiate, there is not one and only one way.

Rather, a lawyer needs to assess each case individually and choose which method might work best for those individual circumstances. These methods include, in reverse order of personal preference, the following:

- *The telephone negotiation.* This may be the only way to negotiate where either geography or cost prohibits other options. It is not the most effective.
- *The snail mail negotiation.* As with telephone negotiations, it may be the only available method where geography or cost prohibits other means. Again, however, it is usually not the most effective. Still, it is more effective than telephone negotiations since it ensures that proposals won't be misunderstood or "lost in translation."
- *The two-sided face-to-face negotiation.* Where neither of the parties can sit in the same room with each other due to emotional issues, a meeting between the attorneys sans clients may be effective. To maximize the odds of success, the lawyers must have clear directions from the clients and good client control.

- *The four-way meeting.* This method is so common and important that it warrants its own chapter in this book (chapter 10, "The Four-Way Meeting").

Most frequently, a combination of these methods is used; and in some cases, all methods are used at different times.

Although personal meetings are preferable, no method is perfect, and each case merits consideration based on its own circumstances. The following factors are key, not necessarily in this order:

- *The geographical restrictions of the parties and attorneys.*
- *The financial resources of the parties.*
- *The emotional relationship between the parties.*
- *The relationship between the attorneys.* Is the lawyer on the other side one who cannot be trusted? Does the attorney tend to posture during four-way meetings, or is the attorney a calming influence who helps to find solutions?
- *The type of issues involved.* Some issues, such as complex financial calculations, are better understood in writing while others may be easier to discuss verbally.

Of course, one attorney cannot dictate the type of negotiations. At best, an attorney can recommend a method and see if the other side agrees. Again, the method of negotiation is not critical. What is critical is that there *are* negotiations. Therefore, if the other side insists on a certain method, it is better to agree to that method (with rare exceptions, such as the domestic violence victim having to participate in a four-way meeting with an abuser) than to have a standoff with no negotiations at all.

The best example of this type of standoff occurred in the late 1960s when the United States and North Vietnam decided to start peace talks in Paris. For an extended period of time, negotiations were on hold while people were being killed because the United States insisted on a rectangular table at which the Americans would sit next to the South Vietnamese and the North Vietnamese would sit next to the Viet Cong. The other side insisted on a square table to symbolize four separate parties. Finally, an agreement on a round table settled the issue, but perhaps the best suggestion came from an antiwar senator: "Take out all the furniture and make them stand. Maybe that will make them come to an agreement faster!"

Thinking of this incident when it came time to buy furniture for my office, I bought a round table for four-way negotiations. Although certainly no panacea, it does create an atmosphere that is less partisan and divisive—although, there have been sessions where I've been tempted to adopt the senator's suggestion and get rid of the table and chairs altogether!

Making the First Offer

Once again, there are two schools of thought on making the first offer. Attorneys Gilbert Feibleman and Paul Saucy explained it this way:

> [T]here is a split of opinion as to whether it is useful to make the first offer. Your initial offer may have been substantially better than expected and may spur settlement while creating a sense of fairness. However, it is likely that the party who makes the first offer is also likely to make the first concession.[1]

It is indeed nice to see what the other side has to offer first and then decide whether to bracket your counterproposal (by creating an acceptable middle ground); provide an extreme proposal (especially if the first proposal is extreme); or make a ballpark proposal, leaving little, but still some, room for moving. However, if the other side tends to take extreme positions, it can be advantageous to make the first proposal and show where the ball exists. The concept of "anchoring" (to be discussed further in the chapter on game theory, chapter 18, "Divorce Settlements and Game Theory") can be used to your advantage in making the first offer.

As with the other basic concepts discussed in this chapter, although there are pros and cons to making the first offer, the only true error is not to negotiate at all. So, assess the individual circumstances of the case and don't stand on ceremony. If the other side wants to make the first proposal, let it. If the other side won't make a proposal, then you do so. One way or the other, get the process started.

---

1. Gilbert B. Feibleman & Paul Saucy, *The Art of Divorce Settlement Negotiations*, FAM. L. REV. 1, 13 (Summer 2010).

Simplifying the Process

At the outset of negotiations (and maybe even before negotiations), there are two simple agreements that lawyers should try to make with the other side. Both are very basic but can save the clients money without sacrificing substance—a rare combination.

The first is to list all assets and debts in the same order as the other side. Of course, in cases with few assets, this is not necessary; but it greatly increases efficiency if there is a large number of assets or liabilities. The concept is simple: it does not matter what asset is listed first; it is simply easier to refer to Item #27 in the process of negotiations than to refer to, say, an account number. Not uncommonly, the list of assets and liabilities in a case will be different at the end than it was at the beginning. For example, property may be sold, or even turn out to have been sold long ago. Better yet, but more uncommonly, a debt will be paid in full. In those cases, lawyers will simply delete the asset or liability and leave the line on the spreadsheet blank to avoid having to renumber all of the following items. Having an identical list makes negotiations easier for both parties.

Second, all numbers should be rounded off—and I don't mean to the nearest dollar. At an absolute minimum, all numbers should be rounded off to the nearest $10, and that amount should be increased depending on the size of the estate. In a large case, rounding off to the nearest $1,000 is quite proper. After all, if there is an even number of assets and liabilities, such rounding off should result in the same arithmetic at the end. Even if there is an odd number, the resultant risk is less than the cost of trying to calculate the exact equalization number. In any case, there is a certain amount of slippage, where the cost of making perfect calculations would exceed the difference of "round ups" and "round downs." Again, using round numbers in negotiations makes the process easier and more efficient.

Order of Negotiation

Once again, there are different schools of thought. One school believes that you should start with the most difficult issues on the theory that once they are concluded (*if* they are concluded), the easy ones will fall into place. The other theory, set forth by C. Terrence Kapp in *The Joy of Settlement*, is to start working on the easy ones and then progress to the more difficult ones. His theory is that by resolving issues at the outset, a tone for resolution is established. If you start with the difficult issues, according to Kapp, there is a greater likelihood of getting bogged down and making no progress whatsoever.[2]

The problem is that in many cases the issues are interrelated. Therefore, the choice of order should rely on the nature of the issues. If the degree of interrelation is large, then it makes sense to start with the more difficult issues, and the result will drive resolution of the easier ones. The inverse, however, is not true. If the issues are completely or largely severable, then Kapp is correct. Reaching a stalemate early is not helpful; but if it happens, put that issue on ice and move onto the next one.

Big Picture versus Little Picture

Some cases are conducive to a "big picture" settlement, which provides a total comprehensive settlement without specific valuations of each asset—a colleague of mine calls it "down and dirty." In a "little picture" negotiation, the parties compare valuations on every asset and liability.

A big picture negotiation is easier to conduct in smaller cases than in larger cases. In fact, in many small cases, there is no sense negotiating in any other manner since there really is no little picture at all.

Even where a big picture proposal may work, however, it usually needs to include some little picture features, if for no other reason than for malpractice avoidance. Most cases, as a result, start out as little picture negotiations to get a feel for the ballpark. Both sides compile a list of all assets and debts and calculate an equalizer. If both sides can agree on distribution of the assets, i.e., who gets what, they can then compare the equalizer. If the equalizers are close to one another, they can split the difference and the case is settled. In such a negotiation, both sides may never agree on how they got to that number—they just agree on the number.

Anecdote interlude: Once, following this procedure, the other lawyer and I agreed on the list of assets and debts and the distribution. When we compared equalizers, however, mine was actually more

---

2. C. Terrence Kapp, *Negotiating from Easy to Difficult*, in THE JOY OF SETTLEMENT 93, 95 (Gregg Herman ed., 1997).

favorable to the other side and vice versa. Guess what? Right! The case settled!

Of course, big picture negotiations can be accomplished with few valuations or even without any at all. However, the extent to which valuations are waived is the extent to which the lawyer should paper his file with such documentation as may be necessary to defend that lawyer if the client later criticizes the representation.

Summary

These are some of the basic concepts of divorce settlement negotiations. No hard-and-fast rules are set forth here for two reasons. One, a lawyer has total control over only one quarter of the negotiations with some control over another quarter. In fact, sometimes the more one side tries to influence the settlement procedure, the more the other side resists, if for no other reason than to be ornery. Second, every case needs to turn on its own specific circumstances, including the nature of the issues, the relationship of the parties, the attorney on the other side, and other factors. Therefore, lawyers should not get stuck in a rut and should be open to possibilities. The only mistake is to not negotiate at all.

Timing 3

Settling a divorce case is similar to trying to land a jet on an aircraft carrier. You are not aiming for where the ship is now as it will have moved by the time you arrive. So you plot a course for where you think it might be by the time you get there, taking into account its general course, wind and wave conditions, and your ability to fly and navigate. Meanwhile, you make periodic midcourse corrections to keep on track. If you overshoot or undershoot the ship, you crash. The goal is to time your arrival for a smooth landing.

Stages of Divorce Proceedings

Most divorce cases seem to follow a general pattern. First, everyone is angry and revenge laden. The lawyers get frequent calls. The animosity is so great that one wonders how these people ever were intimate with each other and pledged, sometimes before their deity, to stay together "until death do us part." The transition seems to occur when the first bills from the attorneys arrive, which inform the clients that their retainers are used up. Then, both parties begin the process of coming to the realization that fighting only enriches their attorneys while harming their children. And the settlement process begins.

Of course, not all cases proceed in such a chronological fashion; but for those that do, it is remarkable the extent to which the pattern mirrors Elisabeth Kübler-Ross's famous "five stages of grief": denial, anger, bargaining, depression, and acceptance.[1] Often, the pattern includes a couple of extra stages uniquely associated with divorce.[2] Thus, many couples start with denial and proceed through anger, fear, guilt, and bargaining (although not the good type of settlement-based bargaining) until both parties reach acceptance.

Such stages of grief are not surprising; after all, a divorce is the death of a marriage. The goal of divorce lawyers should be to provide a dignified funeral.

Importance of Timing

Trying to negotiate when both parties accept the end of the marriage is far easier than when they are in the anger stage. It is not always possible to time settlement negotiations accordingly, but lawyers need to recognize the concept of timing and try to adapt the course of negotiations to the psychological arc of the parties.

I discuss in this book the art of the lawyer listening to the client, but the reverse is true as well: the client must listen to the lawyer. Overly emotional clients, whether due to anger, fear, or some other emotion, do not hear what the lawyer is saying—even if they are listening. All lawyers with a few years of experience have heard clients ask for an explanation of a settlement agreement *after they have signed it* even though the lawyer explained it frequently during the course of negotiations. People consumed with emotions are not absorbing the advice that they are getting. It's no wonder family law is one of the leading areas for ethics complaints and malpractice lawsuits. It is not that family law attorneys commit more ethics violations or malpractice than other lawyers. Rather, the timing of negotiations does not always

---

1. ELISABETH KÜBLER-ROSS, ON DEATH AND DYING (1997).
2. *See, e.g.*, Pauline H. Tesler & Peggy Thompson, *The Emotional Stages of Divorce*, WOMANS DIVORCE (2012), http://www.womansdivorce.com/emotional-stages-of-divorce.html (last visited Oct. 25, 2012).

afford the parties an opportunity for detached contemplation of their options and selection of the one that best suits their circumstances.

Timing Issues

In some cases, timing, although important, is a moot issue.

For example, sometimes timing is not a consideration (although it should be!) because of lack of control over timing: the system does not allow an individual client as much time as needed to work through the emotional issues. Courts control their calendars, and some are faster than others. Although some judges will allow the parties time to emotionally adjust to a divorce, some will not and will force matters—even if neither party is ready. Worse, there are some clients for whom there will *never* be enough time because they are not progressing through the stages of grief, sometimes due to a mental disorder or substance addiction.

Timing also may have to take a backseat to proper discovery. Although, as discussed in a separate chapter of this book (chapter 6, "Disclosure"), the parties should cooperate by voluntarily and promptly exchanging all necessary financial information, appraisals (especially business appraisals) can take quite some time to be done properly. In such cases, the lawyers need to carefully estimate the anticipated timeline so that their clients can adjust their expectations accordingly. When I hire an appraiser, I ask for the latest possible date when I can expect the appraisal; I far prefer my client to be pleasantly surprised by getting it earlier than frustrated that it had not arrived on time.

Timing also does not help a client whose sole goal is destruction. This type is exemplified by the allegory of the crocodile and the scorpion: A scorpion asks a crocodile for a ride across a river. The crocodile tells the scorpion that its sting is fatal to him, to which the scorpion replies, "But I can't swim, so if I sting you, I will die as well." This makes sense to the crocodile, so he lets the scorpion hop on top of him. Halfway across the river, the scorpion stings the crocodile. As the crocodile is drowning, taking the scorpion with him, he asks the scorpion why it stung him, dooming them both. The scorpion's reply: "Because I am a scorpion."

There are scorpions out there that do nothing but sting, and there is no effective settlement strategy for such people (at least, of which I am aware). But, fortunately, human scorpions are rare. Most human beings will eventually make rational decisions consistent with their own best interests, even if they behave irrationally for a period of time. And settlement is the rational choice for all divorcing parties.

Recognition of the Right Time

How, then, to recognize and take advantage of the right time?

First, be patient. Just because a client is consumed with anger at an early stage does not mean that settlement will be impossible later.

Second, pay attention. Lawyers need to meet periodically with such clients and, in addition to listening to them, watch them. It is widely accepted that communication is at least 80 percent nonverbal. What nonverbal cues is the client giving you? Is the body posture appropriate? Is the client fidgeting? If you ask the client to repeat something you said, can he do so accurately? If the client is not hearing what you are saying, it is probably not time for settlement.

Third, observe the dynamics of the interaction of opposing counsel and his client at a four-way meeting. At one such session of which I was a part, the opposing counsel (who was one of those busy lawyers with more cases than he could effectively handle) kept calling his client by the wrong name. Worse, the wrong name was the correct name for my client's girlfriend. The wife was clearly so angry with her lawyer that it was apparent that negotiations that day would be futile, and I terminated the session.

Fourth, although the anecdote about the crocodile and the scorpion is, of course, not an example of typical human behavior, sometimes you can just sense whether a settlement is ripe that day. Trust your instincts. If it feels right, go for it: make the proposal that should lead to resolution. If it doesn't feel right—if the atmosphere is poisonous—you may want to keep the proposal in your pocket for a better time.

Testing the atmosphere is no more an exact science for settlement negotiations than it is for meteorology. And you do not have complete control over the timing: both your client and the other side have a say. Still, to the extent that you have any control, once you have sufficient information to begin discussions, try to do so. Sometimes emotions need to be prodded to catch up to reality. When uncertain, it is better to start the process and run the risk of having to put it on ice for a while than to run out of time to negotiate effectively because you waited too long.

Summary

A lawyer needs to be sensitive to when both parties are willing to make the compromises necessary to get to an agreement. Although the timing is not always within a lawyer's control, lawyers should not push a settlement process for which one of the parties is not prepared. On the other hand, lawyers should not delay starting the process until it's too late and a trial date changes all of the variables in the equation. The important thing to keep in mind is that there are no wrong times to settle a case—but there are better times and worse times.

Controlling Emotions 4

When meeting with a client to discuss making a settlement proposal, it seemed that the client was not focusing on the key issues, such as the settlement options, risks of trial, and costs of litigation. When I asked the client if she was tuned in, she smiled sweetly and asked if she could explain what she would really like. "Of course," I responded, "that's the purpose of our meeting."

"Well, I really don't care about what I end up with—or the costs. I'll be pleased to pay you," she said. "What I would like to see is for you to hurt that son of a bitch the way he hurt me."

She spoke without a tinge of anger in her voice—but there was no mistaking the deep emotion punctuating every word.

If there is one common theme in this book, it is the effect that emotions play in getting to a win-win settlement in a divorce case. Of course, there are emotional aspects involved in many other areas of law as well, but emotions seem to be at their height when issues of family are involved. Although there is a tendency for lawyers to either ignore the emotions or have the client simply "get over it," the former is doing a disservice to the client and the latter is simply not going to happen. Therefore, it is impossible to discuss settlement negotiations in divorce without paying particular attention to the role played by emotions.

Emotions: The Positives and the Negatives

In their book, *Beyond Reason: Using Emotions as You Negotiate*, Roger Fisher (of "Fisher and Ury" fame) and Daniel Shapiro recognized that emotions can, of course, be obstacles to negotiating; however, they also found that emotions can be a positive asset.[1]

Clearly, emotions can be a substantial impediment to negotiations. As outlined by Fisher and Shapiro, negative emotions can do the following:

- Divert attention from substantive matters
- Damage relationships
- Provide information that can be used to exploit the other party
- Lead to bad decisions

Yet, emotions can also be a great asset. Positive emotions can do the following:

- Increase listening and learning of the other side's concerns
- Establish a cooperative working relationship

Dealing with Emotions

So, how should family lawyers deal with the emotions inherent in their field?

Certainly, recommending counseling for clients is a good idea, but it is not a complete answer. Some lawyers seem to think differently; however, counselors are not miracle workers. At best, counseling takes time. There is even some question about the efficacy of counseling during a divorce when emotions are highest. In any event, counseling can be of assistance in managing a client's emotions, but it is not the total answer.

---

1. Roger Fisher & Daniel Shapiro, Beyond Reason: Using Emotions as You Negotiate (Penguin Group 2005).

Rather, lawyers in this field need to be prepared to handle an emotional client and, ideally, channel the emotional energy into something positive rather than something negative.

Below are several suggestions on how to do this.

Listen

Sometimes clients just want to be heard. Even though most states are "no fault," many clients are not emotionally there. If no one is listening, clients can feel stifled and frustrated. As attorneys Gilbert Feibleman and Paul Saucy noted,

> *[l]istening clues you to what is needed as you begin to offer guidance, direction or redirection. Remember, too, that you may have heard the same story a hundred times, but this is a first for the client. Avoid the temptation to pigeonhole the client's problem into the ready-made scenario that you already have the answers for. Each case is unique and the later negotiations will involve complex, intertwining goals and concerns with a healthy spicing of emotion thrown in.*[2]

Listening is an art; and, quite frankly, most lawyers are not particularly good at it because our profession teaches us to be advocates—to be assertive rather than impassive. However, there are techniques available for those of us who are more proactive and find it difficult to simply sit back and listen:

- Occasionally summarize what the client is saying. For example, say, "Let me interrupt a moment and make sure I'm understanding you." Then follow this statement with a summary.
- Ask questions.
- Don't try to think of a response—concentrate on what you are being told. Pretend that you are not allowed to talk.
- Practice with friends and family. With sufficient practice, this can become a habit. (Side benefit: This may help with relationships in your personal life.)
- Prepare a script of questions designed to elicit responses. The questions should be relatively open-ended.

---

2. Gilbert B. Feibleman & Paul Saucy, *The Art of Divorce Settlement Negotiations*, FAM. L. REV. 1, 8 (Summer 2010).

In fact, according to Feibleman and Saucy, "'[l]istening' does not mean that the lawyer should sit quietly through the entire first interview."³ Rather, they continued,

> *[d]epending on the client, you may want to listen for the first ten to fifteen minutes without anything more than an occasional affirmative response to let the client know that you are attentive. A typical statement in the first fifteen minutes would be: "He said what?" "Was that the first or the second time that happened?" "How did you respond?" It is the affirmation that you are listening which is important, not the answer. Gradually insert yourself into the discussion by guiding the discussions to the areas that will make an actual difference in your case. You should be doing all of the talking by the end of the hour. By then you are using what you have heard to "take charge" while guiding the client.*⁴

Have a Ready Supply of Kleenex

I tell clients that my firm, being a divorce firm, buys Kleenex by the gross and that I never worry about clients who cry as they describe the deterioration of a marriage from someone they once loved (and may still love)—but I sometimes worry about clients who don't cry. (Depending on the sense of humor of the client, I sometimes note that the only time to worry is if the lawyer is the one doing the crying!)

Validate the Emotions

Don't tell clients, either verbally or nonverbally, that their emotions are inappropriate or wrong. Emotions are what they are—they are neither right nor wrong. Listen, understand, and appreciate. Then, you can explain what *no fault* means and, if necessary, the value of counseling.

Provide Assurance

Much of a client's emotion simply arises from fear. Fear of the unknown. Fear of being alone. Fear of the legal process—or even dealing with a lawyer (lawyers don't have the greatest reputations).

---

3. *Id.*
4. *Id.*

Assurance is different than a guarantee. We don't know what the results will be, but we do know from experience that most clients survive their divorce and are in a better place afterward. They need to know that they will get there, too, but that it will take some time and patience. Here is an analogy that I sometimes relate to clients who do not think that they can survive a divorce:

> *I heard a story once that God told people that he was going to bring another flood, but this time there would not be time to build an ark—the rains were already coming. People reacted in a variety of ways. Some grabbed hammer and nails and started building an ark even though it was too late. Others argued with God. Some curled up in the corner and cried. Others emptied their liquor cabinet to deaden the coming pain. But others—the healthy ones—went to the library to check out books on how to live under water.*
>
> *I'm sorry, but it appears that for your marriage, the rains are coming, and it's too late to save it (build an ark). Arguing, drinking, and crying are not productive. So, you are going to emotionally find a way to live with this experience until the rains stop.*

Provide a Long-Term Strategy

Soldiers in a war concentrate on merely staying alive. They do not have the luxury of planning their homecoming while bullets are whizzing overhead. Their choices are to shoot back or simply keep their heads down.

Divorcing couples are in a similar situation. Therefore, we need to provide the homecoming scenario for our clients—the homecoming being their postdivorce life. We cannot, of course, promise them that it will be perfect—or even satisfactory. But we can assure them that we are planning for it.

For divorcing couples, the options during the "war" are not pretty. Shooting back leads to an escalation of violence. Keeping their heads down does not provide forward momentum. Thus, in each case, the lawyer needs to reassure the client that there is a strategic plan in place designed for long-term life improvement. And the lawyer needs to continually remind the client to work toward that goal, whatever it might be in an individual case.

Don't Get Sucked into the Emotional Conflict

Remember, you are a professional. Act like it. Taking on the emotions of your client through attack letters or, even worse, verbal attacks on the other side are counterproductive.

Avoiding getting sucked in is not always as easy as it sounds. We tend to like our clients—or, at the very least, we like getting paid by them. Their anger can be contagious. But it is not effective.

One way of avoiding getting sucked in is the twenty-four-hour rule: no letter that you draft is sent out until you have reread it twenty-four hours later, pretending that you are the other attorney. Is it likely to elicit a childish playground response of "Oh, yeah?" or rather a positive response?

A faster method of screening your communications (these days, often e-mail rather than letters) is to ask a staff member to read it through first.

Summary

Divorce can be a very scary, even terrifying, time for people. It is said that the most stressful things in life are a change in residence, a change in employment, a change in marital status, and a change in health. It is not uncommon to find that divorcing parties have multiple—and sometimes all of these—stresses.

As a result, much as we would like to focus only on the substance of the issues, we need to give clients a chance to express their emotions, hopefully in a controlled setting. Let them vent, at least a little. Show that you are listening and that you care. As a result, the end result, even if it is only a business solution, will be lot easier for the client to accept.

Preparing the Client for Settlement 5

As with everything else in life, preparation is key—preparing the client for what settlement negotiations entail.

My late partner, Leonard Loeb, used to say that his toughest negotiations were with his own clients. Rather than making unreasonable promises to a potential client in order to get the business, good lawyers should explain at the outset that settlement requires compromise and that compromising means giving something up. Specifically, what and how much is given up are what negotiations are all about. Clients and potential clients need to understand this concept from Day 1 (in other words, when the lawyer and client first "meet," whether on the telephone, in person, or online).

Convincing a Client to Negotiate

The concept, although simple enough in the abstract, becomes complicated when mixed with the high degree of emotions inherent in a divorce. Included in these emotions is a lack of trust, usually with a good historical basis. I once had a client tell me that she would not agree to any settlement that would be acceptable to her husband because he was so devious, i.e., that if he was willing to accept a settlement, it must be slanted in his favor. This distrust (in severe cases, paranoia) needs to be addressed immediately. If the distrust is based on real-life experience (as Henry Kissinger noted, "even a paranoid can have enemies"[1]), the lawyer needs to explain the discovery process, along with its costs. (If the distrust is truly paranoia, settlement may be impossible, in which case the lawyer has to consider whether this is a person whom the lawyer wants to represent.)

Some clients are extremely doubtful that any settlement discussion can be successful. They wonder why they should even try and feel that it would be better to spend the time and resources on preparing for litigation than wasting them on fruitless settlement negotiations. The lawyer's job is to convince the client to make the effort. Depending on the client, several techniques might be employed.

Anecdotes are a good starting point. Lawyers can tell real-life stories (making sure that no names or identifying information is divulged) of similar cases where settlement looked impossible, but, to everyone's surprise, the case settled nonetheless.

Another technique is using quotes from history to emphasize the importance of settlement. For example, when Yitzhak Rabin, Israeli prime minister, was asked in 1993 why he would even try to reach a settlement with his sworn enemies, the Palestinians, he replied, "You don't make peace with friends. You make it with very unsavory enemies."[2] The result was the Oslo Peace Accords—not perfect, but better than war. Another quote with applications to the issue of settlement negotiations in a divorce is one by Winston Churchill: "To jaw-jaw is always better than to war-war."[3]

Some clients can be convinced to negotiate simply by looking at the costs of litigation versus settlement. When the costs of postjudgment

---

1. BrainyQuote, Henry A. Kissinger Quotes, http://www.brainyquote.com/quotes/quotes/h/henryakis115118.html (last visited Oct. 2, 2012).
2. "Quotables," CHI. TRIB. NEWS, Sept. 15, 1993, http://articles.chicagotribune.com/1993-09-15/news/9309150118_1_rabin-israeli-yaron-ezrahi (last visited Oct. 29, 2012).
3. QuotationsBook, Churchill, Winston, http://quotationsbook.com/quote/44971/ (last visited Oct. 2, 2012). This quote is the most common version of Churchill's words; other, similar versions have been published in various sources. *Id.*

motions and appeals are included, the cost differential should be enough to make any rational person want to sit down at the table.

Some lawyers tell their clients that they need to attempt settlement to "prove" to the court that they tried. I tell clients that many times courts have thanked me and the other lawyer for settling a case. I've never had a court thank me for allowing it to hear even an interesting trial. There is a message there. As all lawyers know, courts prefer resolution to conflict, and it is dangerous for a lawyer to have a court even think the trial is due to that lawyer's intransigence.

Some clients believe that even a show of a willingness to settle is a sign of weakness. In certain cases, of course, a show of muscle is necessary to convince the other side that it has something to lose at trial and that, therefore, it should compromise in negotiations. A friend of mine quotes the Latin maxim "Si vis pacem, para bellum," translated as "If you wish for peace, prepare for war." The degree of trial preparation and muscle flexing will vary from case to case, but it should never be a reason to refuse to negotiate. Rather, the lawyer must convince the client that willingness to negotiate is a sign of maturity, which arises from experience and the desire to be a professional. There may be a place for machismo (both male and female) in our legal system, but its place is not in family court.

Preparing Yourself

Before you can prepare the client for settlement, you must prepare yourself. Doing so requires the following:

- Make a list of all issues in the case that will be the subject of negotiations.
- Consider any legal issues involved and do any necessary research before meeting the client so that you are not wasting time.
- Remind yourself of the judge who will be deciding the matter if negotiations fail. If you are unfamiliar with the judge, call a colleague for a reading of how the judge handles cases and, if known, decides issues. If you can, run a search of appellate cases where the judge was either reversed or affirmed.
- Remind yourself of the opposing counsel and his tactics. If you have never had a case with that lawyer before, call a colleague for input.

- Draft an agenda so that you and the client stay on track and cover all necessary issues.

The Client Meeting

This settlement meeting with the client should be in person, if at all possible. Experts tell us that communication is 80 percent nonverbal. Therefore, if an important discussion (and no discussion is more important than this one) is handled over the phone, the lawyer is assessing only 20 percent of the client's reactions and responses—and vice versa. If possible, this should be a stand-alone meeting, which means that the only agenda item is to develop a settlement strategy. Finally, the meeting should be timed close enough to initial settlement negotiations that circumstances won't change to make the discussion stale but not so close that the client won't have time to assess the strategy and be comfortable with it.

The Meeting Agenda

The lawyer should start by explaining the traditional settlement process and rules. The client should be aware of the following concepts, all of which are discussed in more detail elsewhere in this book:

- *Traditional, positional settlement negotiation.* In traditional negotiation, you will take a position higher (or lower) than what your client is really willing to accept without going so high (or so low) that the other lawyer won't take you seriously. This concept, although it seems obvious, needs to be explained to the client, with the degree of explanation dependent on the sophistication of the client.
- *Bracketing.* As discussed in more detail in chapter 7, "Positional Negotiation," in making a proposal—whether an initial proposal or a responsive one—the client needs to be aware of the dangers of bracketing, which means taking positions on opposing sides of some undefined middle point of a financial issue.
- *Prohibition against backward negotiating.* The client needs to understand that once a proposal has been made, unless circumstances dramatically change, every subsequent proposal must

be closer to the other side's position. Failure to do so will be considered backward negotiating, which is bad faith. Although it is not bad faith to give a deadline for acceptance, that is discouraged as it will be perceived as a threat rather than a good faith offer to compromise. Thus, before the meeting ends, make sure you have the client's permission to make the offer with the knowledge that once it's made, it cannot be withdrawn. Sometimes, depending on the client, I request that permission in writing; an e-mail saying "You have the green light" is sufficient.

- *Ethical rules for representing a client's position.* In the chapter of this book on ethical issues (chapter 19, "Ethical Considerations"), I discuss the concept that a lawyer can misrepresent the client's position on settlement. In fact, it is often good practice to do so. It is recommended, however, that the ethics of this misrepresentation be discussed with the client. Nonlawyers can easily be confused about the difference between misrepresenting a client's position and misrepresenting a material fact.
- *BATNA (Best Alternative To a Negotiated Agreement).* No client (or lawyer, for that matter) can objectively assess a settlement without recourse to the possible outcome of a trial. This possibility needs to be explored with the client so that the potential areas of settlement have a basis for comparison.
- *Walk-away point.* Elsewhere in this book, I will discuss the endgame (see chapter 21, "The Endgame"). At the first settlement meeting with the client, however, identifying the "walk-away point" is not necessary and probably premature. At that time, only the concept needs to be discussed. The client needs to be assured that settlement does not mean give, give, give—and then give some more. Rather, there is a point where negotiations stop and trial preparations start (or continue). This walk-away point is a moving target as the closer the realities of trial (including the cost), the more this point moves toward the other side. Thus, do not be doctrinaire about a specific walk-away point but instead make sure that your client knows that it exists and that you will know it when you see it.

Establishing Reasonable Goals

It is common for clients to want to begin negotiations from an unreasonable starting point. They reason that if they don't ask for it, they won't get it. So they ask for the stars and the moon, sometimes losing sight of Planet Earth.

There may be certain times when this strategy serves a purpose (other than placating a client, that is); but in most cases, at the settlement meeting with the client, reasonable goals need to be established. It takes no skill at all to make a ridiculously high settlement offer. What takes skill is making an offer that, while leaving room to negotiate, results in a reasonable response from the other side.

Sometimes role-playing with a client can help. Ask the client, "What is the response you want from the other side?" Hopefully, the answer will be, "A reasonable response." Then ask the client to pretend that she is the other side—and to consider whether a ridiculous proposal would likely result in a reasonable response.

Summary

A person-to-person meeting with your client is essential for a successful negotiation. The agenda for this meeting needs to include a strategy for negotiations and establishing reasonable goals for the client.

Disclosure 6

In any settlement model, full disclosure is important. After all, "reasonable knowledge of relevant facts" is part of the very definition of *fair market value*.[1] In divorce, full and voluntary disclosure is so important to settlement that it warrants a special chapter in this book. Every state, in one manner or another, mandates both parties to make full disclosure of their financial circumstances. Thus, in addition to being good settlement strategy, full voluntary disclosure complies with legal requirements anyway.

Benefits of Full Voluntary Disclosure

In computerspeak, there is "pull" technology, in which data/programming must be requested; and "push" technology, in which data/programming is provided without being asked. In negotiationspeak, pull disclosure is where the party with less knowledge has to ask for it and sometimes compel production; push disclosure is where the party with more knowledge simply provides it without even being asked. Some parties and, unfortunately, some attorneys think that discovery should be governed by pull

---

1. Rev. Rul. 59-60.

disclosure, where the spouse with less information has to find it, like a game of hide-and-seek.

This attitude is not consistent with successful settlement strategies. As one mediation specialist, Yishai Boyarin, noted, if "there is not enough reliable information on the table, the full scope of the interest of the parties cannot be known."[2] And "the interests-based approach can only work if both the parties agree to disclose the information pertinent to the conflict in order to openly engage in finding solutions that provide for mutual gain."[3]

Think of a poker game. Would you play without knowing that there were fifty-two cards in the deck? If you felt that a card was up the dealer's sleeve, the proper strategy would be to simply not play. Similarly, it would be foolish—and, in fact, it would constitute malpractice—to settle a divorce case without having full disclosure from the other side.

Since most family law attorneys represent both men and women and both the monied side and the nonmonied side (of course, in different cases), they are intimately familiar with what information the other side will need to sit down at the bargaining table. Since they know what information the other side will need, why not simply provide it at the outset, before the other side even asks for it?

Voluntary and complete exchange of information is primarily designed to put the other party at ease to negotiate. Of course, this will not happen in every case. In particular, highly paranoid parties will not appreciate the effort. In one such case I handled, when we voluntarily produced substantial information, the wife said to her lawyer, "See? They're trying to put us off the scent." However, even in this case, the effort of providing full voluntary disclosure was worth it: only the wife was paranoid, not her lawyer, who reassured her that the effort was genuine.

In addition to putting the other side at ease, full voluntary disclosure is important because courts are highly impressed when a lawyer makes discovery easy for the other side. When courts are faced with discovery disputes in divorce, they generally do two things, neither of which is good for the party defending discovery. First, unless the request is

---

2. Yishai Boyarin, *Generating Win-Win Results: Negotiating Conflicts in the Drafting Process of the Uniform Collaborative Law Act*, 38 HOFSTRA L. REV. 495, 503 (2009).
3. *Id.* at 502.

outrageous (and sometimes even then!), the court will order in favor of the party requesting the information on the theory that everything in a marriage should be open information. Second, the court will assume that the motion was necessary because someone (guess who?) was trying to hide information.

Methods of Providing Disclosure

The best method of furnishing full voluntary disclosure is to provide not just a financial statement but a fully annotated one with backup information. An annotated financial statement should include tab numbers for each asset and debt. Then, following the financial statement, there should be a corresponding tab with backup information for each item, e.g., a bank statement, retirement plan statement, Kelley Blue Book car appraisal, or whatever is necessary for the other side to ascertain the nature and, if possible, value of that item. If information is not currently available (such as an appraisal on real estate or a business), there should be a blank page after the tab with a note that information will be supplied when available. Then, when information becomes available, it should be provided with instructions regarding to which tab the information belongs.

Since the binder is difficult to replicate, you should make three copies—one for the opposing counsel and one for each party. The binder does not have to be completely paper; since more and more information, such as tax returns, can be provided without killing trees, you can place a flash drive rather than paper behind the tab for certain information.

Speaking of saving paper, an even more efficient means of sharing bank accounts and other information is to simply provide online access. Years ago, a client would take piles of canceled checks to his lawyer if the other side requested to audit the checking account, obligating the lawyer to copy them since all information in a divorce should be immediately available to both parties. Today, lawyers can simply give the other side the information necessary to access the account itself, usually a user ID number and PIN. Of course, it is imperative to remind whichever client is awarded that account to change the PIN after the divorce.

When such information is not available online, you can have your client sign an authorization for whatever institution has the relevant information. The authorization should require that the information be provided to both sides simultaneously and that the authorization will expire upon the granting of the divorce. You should annotate your file to make sure that a letter terminating the authorization is sent out immediately following the divorce. The cost is minimal: I tell clients that it will cost only two first-class postage stamps (one for a self-addressed, stamped envelope to make it convenient for the institution to respond). It would be impossible for the other side to claim that they are being stonewalled when they have permission to get all the information they want when they want it.

Summary

Full voluntary disclosure is important for both sides. If your client has access to necessary information, provide it voluntarily and completely. The sooner the other side has the information they need, the sooner they will be ready to sit down at the table with you and negotiate.

Although providing substantial information in an organized form on a voluntary basis may cost the client more in the short run, it equals out in the long run. First, it will have to be provided anyway. Second, and more important, it will set a stage for negotiations where the script focuses on the substantive issues, not the ancillary ones. And that, of course, is the desired agenda.

Positional Negotiation 7

Traditional negotiation—in divorce as elsewhere—has been described as positional negotiation. In this form, each side typically begins by taking a maximalist, or best-case scenario, position in its favor and then compromising from that position.

Advantages

There are advantages to positional negotiation. It allows parties to establish their best-case scenario and therefore objectify the compromises being made. In many settlements in which the final numbers are agreed upon, both parties have different views on how they got there. It is not uncommon to hear both sides claim that they made all the compromises and the other side made none. When both sides lay out their best-case positions, there is some objective evidence that the other side made movement as well.

Three Positions

Positional negotiation can be broken into three positions: the optimal position, the opening proposal, and the "go-to-hell" point.

The Optimal Position

The easiest of the three positions is usually the optimal position. Where would the client like to end up? If the attorney does not know where the client would optimally and realistically like to end up, how can negotiations even begin? Of course, although the starting point is to identify what, realistically, would make an optimal settlement, the real world usually intrudes—settlements are rarely optimal.

If the optimal position is not realistic, then the lawyer needs to spend more time preparing the client. The lawyer needs to explain to the client that it is highly unlikely that the client will get everything that she wants. Sometimes the client may get nothing that she wants. The optimal position may need to be reexamined from time to time if it is found to be unrealistic.

Often, clients will have a wish list, sometimes prepared by well-meaning friends and relatives. Whether that wish list is realistic as an optimal position is another question. It takes no skill to make a settlement proposal. The skill is making a settlement proposal that might be accepted by the other side, or at the very least taken seriously.

The Opening Proposal

Once an optimal position is identified in positional negotiation, the lawyer works with the client in developing an opening proposal. This position needs to be far enough away from the optimal position to leave room for negotiating but not so far away as to prevent further negotiations.

In terms of monetary considerations, the term *bracketing* is used when clients take positions on opposing sides of a middle point of a financial issue. In positional negotiation, this occurs all of the time. If both parties take reasonable positions, the middle point should be a reasonable compromise. However, there is a substantial danger that negotiators need to keep in mind: the farther the position that one party takes from a reasonable one, the more the middle position is in that party's favor. After all, a common settlement technique is "splitting the difference," so bracketing can reward a party for being unreasonable. Knowing the opposing counsel is important here, but the key is to keep in mind the eventual arithmetic of splitting the difference.

Finding the sweet spot—leaving room for movement while still making a serious proposal—takes planning and thought. Once, a lawyer made an opening proposal to me shortly before trial. The maintenance part of the proposal was for over 100 percent of my client's income. No, there was no question as to my client's actual income: he was an employee and had no control over his income. My client asked me if there was any chance that the court would order maintenance in an amount that exceeded his total income. Upon being assured that could not happen, he directed me not to respond. He felt that by opening negotiations with an absurd proposal, the other side evinced a lack of seriousness about settlement. The case was litigated (with the wife, of course, receiving far less maintenance).

To a certain extent, negotiating is a matter of culture. As a college student, I lived for a year in the Middle East. In that culture, to buy something without haggling first is rude and foolish. Everyone knows that the first offer merely establishes that the market is open. By engaging in the open marketplace on a daily basis, I learned the following rules of negotiation:

- Never make an offer unless you are willing to open the market. Once you make an offer, the item is on the table for discussion. If you really don't want to buy, don't make any offer, no matter how low.
- The seller has more control than the buyer since he knows the cost involved.
- In a perfect negotiation, the buyer will never know how low the seller would have gone, and the seller never knows how high the buyer would have gone.
- As a buyer, don't be afraid to walk away. You can usually go back later.
- If the negotiation is successful, in most cases, the seller will think he got too little and the buyer will think he paid too much, but neither side will feel cheated because they could have always walked away.

The similarity to divorce negotiations should be obvious, although the identities of the "buyer" and the "seller" are not always clear.

The Go-to-Hell Point

The go-to-hell point is, as it sounds, where negotiations stop and trials begin. Although it needs to be discussed and an attempt at identifying it has to be made, the go-to-hell point, unlike the optimal position and the opening proposal, is flexible.

This is true for several reasons. First, circumstances may easily change during the course of negotiations because of additional discovery, economic fluctuations, one side running short on emotional or financial resources, the other side reneging on an offer, or an emotional shift by a client, to name just a few possible scenarios.

However, the most common reason that the go-to-hell point is flexible is the "footsteps of the jury" syndrome, i.e., negotiating seems more appealing as the trial looms closer. As a prosecutor, I rarely offered any significant concessions for a guilty plea for a major felony case. Of course, to the extent that there were any negotiations, it was quite different than in my experience as a divorce lawyer because the prosecutor holds more power than the defendant: all the prosecutor has to lose is the case, in which event the defendant will probably be back eventually anyway; the defendant has his freedom at stake. Yet, I was amazed at the number of times a defendant would change his plea on the doorstep of trial—sometimes literally with the jury walking toward the courtroom.

Several reasons may account for this phenomenon. Fear, of course, is probably primary. The courtroom is a scary place and in a divorce scenario, an expensive one. But reality plays a major role as well. The case will be over—and soon. The choices are whether to throw the dice on someone else making the choices for you or making these tough choices yourself. Soldiers in war say that artillery fire directed at their position has a way of focusing their attention. Similarly, the imminent start of a trial has a way of focusing mental energy on making the necessary compromises to resolve a matter.

Ultimatum versus Compromise

There are lawyers who do not believe in positional negotiation. Some attorneys believe that lawyers should gather all of the necessary information first and then make one reasonable proposal. Others, such as collaborative lawyers, think that "negotiations" as such should be the product of meetings and transparent discussion rather than the give-and-take of negotiations where the initial proposals are not really intended to be accepted.

The problem with the former approach is that making a take-it-or-else proposal is not a proposal at all. It is an ultimatum. Another word for it is *threat*. Although it may intimidate a weaker opponent into acceptance, an ultimatum is more likely to lead to trial.

Below are two different methods of making a proposal:

- *Method A*: Here is our proposal. If you don't accept it, we will go to trial.
- *Method B*: Here is our proposal. If you don't accept it, let us know why and what you feel would be fair.

Which method would bring out the better nature of the other side? Of course, Method A leads to a knee-jerk reaction: "OK, we'll see you at trial." Method B leads to thinking about the offer and considering whether or not it is acceptable; and if it is not acceptable, why it is not acceptable and what counteroffer needs to be made.

Divorce lawyers need to remember that, unlike most other areas of law, in most of their cases the relationship between the parties does not end with the granting of divorce. In addition to the possibility of future litigation, if there are children (whether minor or adult), the parties will have an ongoing relationship in the future. Again, which method is more likely to lead to a positive relationship? Clearly, it is the method that leads to a settlement borne of compromise rather than one borne of threats and ultimatums. The end result may be the same. The method, though, may lead to a different future for the parties.

The other alternative to positional negotiation—transparent negotiation, which is a feature of collaborative law—has merit under the right circumstances. It avoids one of the drawbacks of positional negotiation: one party thinking that the other party "overasked" by making a high opening proposal (or one party thinking that the other party "underoffered"). However, in most cases, the transparent negotiation approach ignores the reality of the emotional expectations of the parties. Most divorcing parties think (usually for good reason) that the other side wants to pay as little as possible or wants to get as much as possible. Of course they do. They didn't hire lawyers to get as poor a deal as possible. Making a high (or low) initial proposal is consistent with this expectation and, therefore, more likely to be taken seriously. Often, when a proposal confounds expectations, the response is suspicion rather than gratitude.

Summary

In positional negotiation, the parties make an opening proposal that is intentionally higher or lower than the optimal position. There is also a go-to-hell position, which is less than optimal but still preferable to trial. As with everything else, each case needs to be assessed on its individual merits to judge whether positional negotiation is appropriate or whether some other methodology should be applied. Where positional negotiation is appropriate—and it is considered appropriate for the vast majority of divorce cases—the lawyer needs to discuss the three positions (opening proposal, optimal position, and go-to-hell point) with the client initially and then continually update them as circumstances warrant.

Negotiating with Opposing Counsel 8

No football team would even think of going into a game without having scouted the opposition. Since most negotiating is done with the opposing counsel present—and sometimes with only the opposing counsel present—it is critical to have a "book" on, or an understanding of, the opposition. Yet lawyers tend to ignore the nature of the opposition and engage in a "one size fits all" strategy. Actually, that is no strategy at all.

The "Book" on Opposing Counsel

Many times, lawyers know the opposing counsel from prior experience. If there are multiple experiences to draw from, you should already know the style of your opposition. If it is your first case with that lawyer, however, you need to consider whether there are unique aspects of that case (an unusually demanding client, for example) that may make the experience with the other lawyer unusual.

If you don't have sufficient experience on your own, the best way to learn the other lawyer's style is, of course, to call other lawyers. Most lawyers don't mind being asked their opinion; in fact, they find it flattering.

If that doesn't work, or if the case is of particular importance, then you should meet the other lawyer one-on-one at the beginning of the case. As my office generally handles significant estates, we have a policy of meeting any new lawyer face-to-face at the beginning of the action. We find that this meeting generally accomplishes two things. First, it lets us get a reading on the other lawyer. Second, it allows the other lawyer to get to know us. We always suggest that this initial meeting be at the other lawyer's office because we're able to get a feel for the opposition simply by looking around. Is the office well organized? Are there files strewn everywhere? What are the lawyer's personal interests? The pictures on the walls and the trophies in a case can tell a lot.

Definitely in small cities—and even in large ones—lawyers tend to end up conducting business with the same lawyers over and over again. One lawyer that I know, therefore, keeps a copy of all settlement letters that he receives so that they are available to point out inconsistencies. Although I question the effectiveness of this as it is always easy to find distinguishing facts among cases, this lawyer believes that it has value in the right case to embarrass some opposing counsel into tempering extreme positions.

Establishing Rapport with Opposing Counsel

The importance of establishing rapport with opposing counsel cannot be overstated. Of all the reasons to go to trial, one particularly bad one would be that two lawyers cannot get along so they don't talk to each other. An even worse reason would be that the lawyers are behaving like gunmen in the Old West, where their goal is to establish credentials by shooting down the opponent. The lawyer's ego should not—EVER—be a reason to go to trial.

Of course, you cannot go too far to the other extreme. The opposing counsel is your adversary and not your friend—a difficult tightrope to walk in those cases where, outside of the matter at hand, the counsel really *is* your friend (see discussion below of the best friend as opposing counsel). Boundaries need to be established and respected.

The Intimidating Negotiator

Some lawyers have an intimidating demeanor. These lawyers tend to be humorless and use ultimatums. They will settle; but before they do so, they will present unbalanced proposals, and the eventual settlement will usually be on the courthouse steps.

The first rule for dealing with intimidating negotiators is not to try to beat them at their game—unless you are better at it. If you are not intimidating by nature, don't try to be an intimidator. Unless this is your style, you do not want to get into a contest of who can intimidate whom.

Rather, the best (only?) effective strategy is to maintain your cool demeanor and allow the intimidators to do their thing. They are going to do so anyway. In their own mind, in fact, they need to intimidate as it is the only method they feel comfortable utilizing. So, you need to let them do it. Don't show fear and don't get angry.

Oftentimes, however, no strategy will work on a one-on-one basis as the intimidator is less interested in settling the case than in "winning" the negotiations (see discussion below of the competitive negotiator). It is with these lawyers that mediators can be a godsend as a good mediator will not be intimidated and can neutralize the intimidator.

One colleague of mine calls intimidating negotiators *bullies* and warns that they may be mentally unbalanced. Bad enough if the parties are mentally unbalanced, but the lawyers? Yes, this can happen. Her suggestion for such circumstances is to be firm but not incendiary. She adds that it would be helpful to have your client in counseling to deal with the increased stress from negotiating with this personality type. I would only add that, many times, I feel that I may need therapy as well!

The Unethical or Untrustworthy Negotiator

Some lawyers (fortunately, few and far between) simply cannot be trusted. Their settlement positions are later withdrawn or even denied. Their word is no good.

Although these lawyers are difficult, settlement is not impossible. Several strategies can be employed.

The first strategy is to put all negotiations in writing. If the other lawyer refuses to send a letter or e-mail with his position, then you must send one confirming your understanding of the offer before even sharing it with the client.

A second strategy is to utilize a mediator. That way, it is more difficult for this type of negotiator to go back on his word or to deny prior proposals. The type of mediator is important. You want a mediator who takes careful notes and is good at details.

A third strategy is to never trade all points too quickly. You need some additional points to trade off (or give up) when the other lawyer tries to pull the rug out from under you. This is a difficult strategy to engage in if the case is rather simple and involves few issues, but there may still be some small item to hold in reserve, even if it is only personal property. The key to this strategy is preplanning, i.e., knowing ahead of time that the other lawyer cannot be trusted and understanding that any agreement is therefore fragile.

The Cooperative versus Competitive Negotiator

A colleague of mine believes that almost all opposing counsel can be classified as one of two types of negotiators: those who negotiate in a cooperative style and those who negotiate in a competitive style. The former understand the concept of compromise, while the latter are trying to "win," similar in many respects to the intimidating negotiator (discussed above). Since you don't have any choice in your adversary, you will have to accept the style of your adversary and adapt your strategy accordingly.

In dealing with the cooperative negotiator, little accommodation is necessary as that lawyer is working toward compromise. However, when negotiating with the competitive negotiator, you must be careful, as with the untrustworthy negotiator (discussed above), not to make too many concessions too soon. It may be helpful with this style of negotiator to keep certain concessions until the end because part of the competition for competitive negotiators is last-minute maneuvering. It is important that you are aware of this style ahead of time: forewarned is forearmed.

The Best Friend as Opposing Counsel

Especially in smaller jurisdictions, the opposing counsel may not be the intimidating, crazy monster but a friend—maybe even a good friend. This is good in the sense that you know what to expect, but it presents other challenges.

Some clients want a lawyer who is their advocate, not in the sense of advocating for their long-term interests but in terms of verifying their emotions. It satisfies a need for certain clients to see their attorney getting in the other attorney's face and even being highly unprofessional.

Of course, good professional attorneys don't do this and will explain to clients why it is not in their best interests for them to do so. Rather, good attorneys, when they sense a client who is looking for what used to be called *zealous advocacy*, explains to clients why that is not their style.

The other extreme is not a good idea, either. It's one thing to be professional, cordial, and even friendly with the opposing counsel. But moderation, as in all things, including this, is usually wise.

Several times in my career, I have received calls from parties who want to change lawyers because they felt their attorney was too friendly with the other lawyer. Sometimes it seemed the party was simply paranoid. Other times, the party simply did not understand that a friendship with the other lawyer is not inconsistent with effective representation.

There is an urban legend that divorce lawyers conspire to run up fees by engaging in unnecessary tactics during representation. Perhaps it does occur on occasion. But in my experience, what is far more common is for attorneys who are friends to "conspire" to resolve cases and save fees for their clients.

Attorney Gerald Babbitt of Columbus, Ohio, noted,

When counsel are friends, the entire discovery process is easier and ultimately less costly to the litigants. In theory, the discovery process is intended to encourage the free exchange of information between counsel without the necessity of court intervention. In practice, however, discovery in domestic cases is difficult. A friendly relationship with your opponent limits those difficulties.[1]

The key to managing this situation is discussion with the client. If the opposing counsel is a friend, reveal that to the client at the outset. Explain to the client how it can benefit him by avoiding misunderstandings and suspicions. I sometimes pose the issue to the client in this way:

If I have to get certain information, would you prefer if I bring a motion that costs time to draft, prepare for, and go to court and draft an order afterward—or simply pick up the phone and call the other lawyer? Either way, I end up with the same

---

1. Interview by Gregg Herman with Gerald Babbitt, Attorney in Columbus, Ohio (2012).

information. The former may be three to four hours of time. The latter is ten minutes. Your decision.

Another risk is jeopardizing the friendship. A frank discussion between friends may help to alleviate any fears or concerns. I will say to a friend, "I promise you that I will never stab you in the back. If I'm going to use a dagger, the stab will be in the front where you can see it and are fully aware of it."

And in a similar vein, a final risk is that the friendship will jeopardize your judgment. If you're unsure of the effect of what you are doing, Babbitt advised, "[s]tep back from the case and analyze it without regard to who is on the other side. If the offer fits within the overall theory and parameters of the case, then extend the offer and do not worry about how your friendship has affected it."[2]

Summary

You don't get to choose the lawyer on the other side, so you need to accept who that person is and adapt your strategy accordingly. Being familiar with that attorney's personality and style, either through experience or research, is key.

---

2. *Id.*

Negotiating with the Pro Se Party 9

A colleague called me once for advice regarding an appeal. He told me that he lost a case against "Attorney Se." Thinking that *Se* was a strange name, I told him that I didn't know any attorneys with that name. He said that the "lawyer's" first name was "Pro."

Pro se parties—parties that defend themselves—are perfectly capable of winning cases, some think even more so than licensed lawyers since some courts bend over backward to protect them. Therefore, the first thought when dealing with a pro se litigant should not be how you are going to win this at trial but what strategies can be employed to avoid the risk of trial.

Negotiation Strategies

There are some lawyers who would argue that this should be the shortest chapter in this book because, according to them, the only effective strategy for dealing with the pro se litigant is . . . DON'T! The fact that this chapter goes beyond that one word emphasizes that I believe not only that negotiating with the pro se litigant is necessary but also that certain strategies need to be applied that are special to that circumstance.

The strategies to be employed largely depend on the nature of the pro se litigant. Although there are limitless varieties, pro se litigants tend to fit into one of the following categories:

- The litigant who truly cannot afford an attorney (the attorney for the other side is retained either due to an economic disparity—it's the lawyer's pro bono case for the year—or because the lawyer made a big mistake in thinking he was ever going to be paid)
- The litigant who is simply trying to save money
- The litigant who has a license to practice law but is violating the "client who represents" himself maxim
- The evil litigant who wants to run up costs for the other side
- The mentally ill litigant

The Impoverished One

This is probably the easiest variety of pro se litigant since no one is evil or seeking an advantage. Rather, the circumstances barely allow one attorney, if even that many. The settlement strategy is simple because (1) no one is being manipulative and (2) well, there is little to negotiate anyway!

It is imperative in this circumstance that the lawyer protect himself from the perception that he is representing both parties. When we get postjudgment calls in cases where one side was pro se, it is not unusual to hear someone say, "One lawyer represented both of us." Of course, if we look at the file, there are notations—often, multiple times—in which the lawyer made clear that he was only representing one party. Nevertheless, whether the nonrepresented party didn't listen or just didn't hear, the party will think that it was being represented.

The disclaimer "I am only representing your spouse" should be made in virtually every communication to the unrepresented party, from the initial letter to the final settlement agreement. The disclaimer should include advice that the nonrepresented party hire its own attorney. Here is some sample language that can be adapted to suit your own style:

> *One lawyer cannot represent both parties in a lawsuit, and a divorce action is a lawsuit. Therefore, I am representing only your spouse and not you. Although I will represent any material facts to you, I have no obligation to give you legal advice,*

so please don't ask me for it. If you feel that anything that I say falls into the area of advice, rather than information, you rely on it at your own peril. It is highly recommended that you retain your own independent legal counselor to give you legal advice and representation.

The Penny Pincher: Penny Wise and Pound Foolish

Do you know anyone who selects a doctor by cost? I've never heard someone say, "I need medical care; let me see who is the least expensive." Yet, many people look for the cheapest representation. And others, although they can afford and need representation, go without a lawyer solely to save money.

In some jurisdictions, the strategy that you should use for dealing with the penny pincher is to advise him that going without representation means having to share in your cost. For jurisdictions that are not good at ordering fee contributions—or where this strategy just doesn't work—the strategy is the same as for the "no funds available" case: do not give legal advice to the nonrepresented party, and make ample use of disclaimers in writing.

The "Fool for a Client"

Among the most frustrating of the varieties of pro se opposing parties is the lawyer who proves the maxim about the lawyer who represents himself: "A lawyer who represents himself has a fool for a client." It is not clear which subvariety is more frustrating: the lawyer who has practiced (or, worse, is practicing) family law or the lawyer who has never practiced in this field. For the former variety, a little bit of knowledge is a dangerous thing. For the latter variety, the lack of experience is a gross deficit.

As with the penny pincher, to the extent that the fool is representing himself to save money, the threat of a contribution may be successful. After all, if the fool is going to be paying for a lawyer one way or the other, chances are he would prefer to pay his own lawyer rather than the spouse's lawyer.

The Evil One

As all lawyers know from bitter experience, at the far end of the spectrum are some pro se litigants who are pure evil. They are rare, but they do exist. The evil manifests itself in a variety of ways: ignoring the law, ignoring court orders, taking unreasonable positions, engaging in intense litigation, and even worse ways.

There is not any effective means of dealing with pure evil. Of course, if possible, the best strategy is to avoid it as no case is worth the aggravation. If you cannot avoid it—or didn't recognize it until it was too late—you need to minimize the harm to your client (and yourself). Under no circumstances should you play the evildoer's game: you will lose because he is better at that game than you are. Your best hope is that the legal system does what it is designed to do, which is to punish evildoers and protect their victims. Since the legal system does not always do this effectively, reliance on it is a fallback position. Avoidance is the best strategy.

The Mentally III One

The mentally ill pro se litigant is actually a subset of the evil one (or is it the other way around?); and, as with the evil one, there is no perfect strategy. In fact, I'm not sure there is any effective strategy.

Sometimes the best you can do is not to make things any worse, and this may be one of those times. How do you avoid making things worse? First, recognize the problem and your inability to fix it. Second, avoid being crazy yourself. The court (and your client) does not need two crazy lawyers, even if one is only acting that way in retaliation. So, if you are caught in this impossible situation, maintain your professionalism and demeanor at all times. Create a contrast, not a duplicate.

Risks in Negotiating with Attorney Se

Although there are risks in everything we do in life, there are special risks when the other side is not represented. Of course, other attorneys may misrepresent what you say or propose, but in situations in which the other side has a license to practice law, at least there are rules that are supposed to apply, which mitigates the risk. No such rules apply with the pro se opposing party, which makes it important to always have a witness (even if it's just your client) whenever you meet with the pro se party.

Attorney Sondra Harris noted that

> *it is important not to overreach or try to make an agreement "too good" when negotiating with an unrepresented party. A court will set aside an agreement if the court feels that it is unfair as opposed to simply being a "bad" deal. Thus, a lawyer must strike a balance between getting as much as possible for the client and still striking a fair, good-faith settlement that will stand up to court scrutiny.*[1]

Due to the increased risk of a three-way meeting going bad, Harris advised having ground rules, preferably in writing, agreed upon prior to such a meeting. These ground rules would include starting and ending times, no rude behavior, an agenda, and any rules of conduct specific to the circumstances.[2]

Another risk is that the pro se party is simply feeling you out for compromises and then will take any proposed deal to a lawyer to see if it can be sweetened. If that seems to be the plan, don't back yourself into a corner with any proposed settlement. Rather, if a settlement seems to be near but the pro se party seems to be leaving some room for late maneuvering, don't make your last offer. Rather, leave some money on the table for future negotiating so that you can make some final compromises and still end up with an acceptable settlement.

Summary

Whether rightly or wrongly, the law allows a person to represent himself even if he is a fool for doing so. These are almost always difficult situations and must be dealt with carefully so that your client gets the best representation possible while you maintain your dignity and professionalism at all times.

---

1. Interview by Gregg Herman with Sondra Harris, Attorney in New York (2012).
2. *Id.*

The Four-Way Meeting 10

Although four-way meetings are not unheard of in other areas of law, they are far more common in family law cases. For one thing, the parties know each other intimately. Second, many of the issues involved, such as children, are not really legal issues at all but ones that should be discussed and resolved by the parties directly. And, most important, as frequently stated in this book, the emotional issues in family law tend to cloud everything else. As a result, getting the parties to face each other can be a good way (or a disastrous way!) to get to the heart of the matter.

Economic reality plays a huge role in most family law cases.[1] Frequently, it is unclear if proposals are being "lost in translation" between attorneys and the parties. The fear of the unknown lawyer can also be an issue: parties sometimes assume that any offer from the other side must be made with the intention of manipulating rather than making a compromise. In these instances, a four-way meeting

---

1. There was a judge in my jurisdiction, Hon. Patrick Sheedy, who used to say, "Only three couples in this county can afford a divorce, and I don't see any of them in court today."

can efficiently put all parties on the same page regarding any proposals and can sometimes convince a party that the other side is sincere about resolution. Therefore, in this chapter, I'll discuss some of the issues that these meetings involve and some possible strategies to produce better results.

When to Meet and When Not to Meet

Although the four-way meeting can efficiently resolve many cases, like all settlement tactics, it is not one size fits all. There are signs to look for when considering when such a meeting might work—or not.

A four-way meeting is likely to be productive when the following conditions are present:

- Both parties are willing to make compromises to reach resolution.
- The opposing attorney has a settlement mentality.
- Full discovery has been completed, or the remaining questions can be answered as part of the agenda for the meeting.

On the other hand, four-way meetings are less likely to be productive when the following conditions are present:

- Either party has physically or emotionally abused the other party.
- The opposing counsel likes to perform to impress his client.
- Either party has not been cooperating with making a full disclosure of all necessary information.

If any of the negative factors are present, a five-way meeting with a mediator present, rather than a four-way meeting, might be an effective means of reaching a settlement.

Whose Office?

The first sign of a power struggle is a conflict over whose office will be the meeting place for the first meeting. Some compare this issue to home-court advantage in a basketball game.

Although there are similarities, there may be advantages to having the first meeting in the other lawyer's office. For one, if the meeting does not go well due to the other party (or lawyer) misbehaving, you can walk out. That's difficult to do if the meeting is in your own office! Second, most cases will take more than one meeting to resolve all issues. In those cases, the first meeting tends to be more of a "sniff" meeting (think of two dogs meeting for the first time). The second meeting then becomes more substantive and meaningful. If the first meeting is on "enemy turf," you have the right to insist that the second and more important one is on your turf. Hopefully, if there is a third or more meetings, there is enough familiarity with the location and the people involved to negate advantages either way.

So what happens if both lawyers want that first meeting in their own office (they've both read my book!)? It's not worth fighting about; it's more important that the meeting take place than that it take place in a certain setting. It's for situations like this that coins have two sides (that is the reason, isn't it?).

One colleague pointed out that some lawyers use positioning to try to gain a psychological advantage if the meeting is in their office. Positioning can include giving the other lawyer a lower chair or a seat facing sunlight. Her suggestion is to study the situation *before* sitting down and make sure that you are comfortable with the arrangements; if not, insist on changing them. If the lawyer refuses, you have a good clue that the agenda for the meeting is less about reaching a compromise than about intimidating you into surrender.

Preparing for the Meeting

An agenda, preferably in writing, is essential to staying on task. Whether proposals are exchanged ahead of time or not will depend on the individual circumstances, but it is essential to have a list of issues in play. The agenda and the issue of whether or not proposals will be exchanged should be part of a premeeting discussion between the attorneys.

It is sometimes helpful to set an ending time for the meeting. This can keep the attention focused on the issues if the discussion starts to drift.

And, of course, each attorney needs to meet with his client prior to the meeting to discuss, at a minimum, the agenda, the schedule, and the importance of acting in a civil manner during the meeting even if provoked to act differently.

The Meeting

A short speech by the lawyers at the meeting often can set an appropriate atmosphere for settlement. Such a speech would go along these lines:

> *We are here today to try to resolve this matter. We are not here to try to criticize or chastise the other side. If we are going to do that, we'll do that in court while the judge is listening. Today is to see if there is common ground to avoid having to do that. Therefore, if there is anything that I say that you view as an attack, please let me know immediately so I can retract it.*

It is preferable if the attorneys can agree in advance to such a speech and can in some sense give the speech jointly so that it does not appear that one attorney is attempting to hijack the meeting.

Usually, it is preferable to make a list of issues to be resolved without even discussing the substance of any of them. Then prioritization comes into play. Most times, it is helpful to discuss the easier items first to set an atmosphere for settlement and avoid getting bogged down, or even stalemated, early. If an early issue becomes sticky, don't get into it too deeply—put it aside for the moment and move on to the next item on the agenda.

Misbehavior should not be tolerated, but it does not have to terminate the meeting. If it becomes clear early on that the other side's agenda is less about compromising and more about attacking you and/or your client, you should suggest a recess. Something along the following lines might be helpful:

> *Those comments are really not moving us toward a resolution. Let me suggest that we take a short break. My client and I are going to step out. Can I ask that you discuss whether we can continue this meeting productively or not?*

Such a time-out can prevent emotions from escalating out of control and inform the other side that if the bad conduct continues, the meeting will be a total waste of time and money. Of course, if the time-out does not work, the meeting should be terminated.

Concluding the Meeting

There are three potential scenarios for the end of a four-way meeting: no progress at all, some progress, or full settlement.

If you really cannot resolve any issue, no matter how small, at a four-way meeting, it is time to consider another strategy altogether. Some cases are better settled through a mediator, an exchange of letters, or even a two-way meeting, i.e., either the lawyers alone or the parties without their lawyers.

More commonly, there is some, but not full, resolution at the end of a four-way meeting. Especially if the parties are meeting the other lawyer for the first time and are only now exchanging proposals, they may need some time to consider their options. Not everyone is capable of making instant decisions—and sticking to them. You need to know your client (and try to know the other side) to assess whether some time for contemplation is necessary. After all, it does no one any good, and potentially a lot of harm, for someone to pull the plug on a possible deal.

If an agreement is reached, it should be placed in writing immediately. If possible, this should be done before leaving the four-way meeting, with copies given to everyone. Alternatively, one lawyer should take responsibility for drafting a settlement memo and disseminating it as soon as possible. Sometimes the agreement doesn't last because a settlement looked different on paper than it sounded; there was not a meeting of the minds on the exact terms; or, not infrequently, one of the parties didn't get approval from a third person, such as a parent or a friend. Don't try to ram the agreement down anyone's throat. If it's a good agreement, representing reasonable compromise by both parties, it will last.

Summary

Four-way meetings can be a highly effective and efficient means for negotiating divorce cases. However, they run the risk of being highly destructive as well. To maximize the chances of success, a lawyer has to carefully consider the dynamics of the case, including the relationship between the parties and between the attorneys. The meeting should not take place without advance planning, including, at a minimum, an agreed-upon agenda for discussion.

The Role of the Judge 11

Although this is a book primarily for lawyers, there is a role that courts can play in promoting settlement. Of course, there may be little lawyers can do to influence judges to facilitate settlement (other than buy them a copy of this book!). But, to the extent that lawyers are involved with bench/bar committees or have informal discussions with judges, they have some opportunities. This chapter is designed to share some thoughts on how judges can promote the settlement process, thoughts that can be shared should the opportunity arise.

For the most part, asking judges to promote settlement is the proverbial example of preaching to the choir. With few exceptions, judges, for good reason, dislike trying family law cases. Some of that is surely due to the destruction that the cases wreak on the family and the consequent long-term harm to children. Part of that is surely due to the restrictions in the nature of the orders that judges are empowered to make, as opposed to the flexibility afforded the parties in a settlement. And some of the reluctance may be due to difficulty in utilizing the rules of evidence to ferret out the truth in complex family relationships.

Facilitating Settlement

Let me suggest that the judge's role, trite as it might sound, is to facilitate settlement at the earliest possible time with the best chance of a lasting solution in the most cases possible. There are three factors that affect whether a judge can substantially facilitate settlement of family law cases on a systematic basis.

Leadership

Leadership starts with judges following the same rules of civility and professional conduct that they require of lawyers and parties who appear in court. One judge before whom I used to appear would start every court session informing everyone of the remaining number of days before he would be allowed to transfer to a different branch. *Hey, Judge, it's your job! If you don't like it, go into private practice like the rest of us!* Worse, some judges publicly complain about their low compensation in comparison to what they believe the lawyers are earning. Even if they are correct (and they are probably not), the attitude of disaffection for their job is not conducive to an atmosphere of compromise and civility that promotes settlement.

There is, certainly, an opposite point of view. A judge who is erratic in ruling and cranky on the bench may promote settlement by simply intimidating everyone in court. Yet, a settlement borne of fear is not the ideal settlement. Rather, the ideal settlement is one crafted from a careful consideration of options and risks with compromises by both sides. A settlement borne of mutual fear of the court is not consistent with this goal.

Part of leadership should be learning the principles of mediation and applying those principles whenever possible at hearings, informal conferences, and management conferences. Judicial education courses should teach these principles regularly. Learning these principles does not mean that judges should become mediators; after all, the court needs to maintain its impartiality. But, like a mediator, there is nothing wrong with a judge giving some guidance on issues. The court needs to explain to the parties that it is not predeciding any issue and that if the matter does not settle, the court will start with a tabula rasa and base its decision solely on the evidence produced at trial. Still, even with such a warning, courts should not hesitate to adopt some of the principles of dispute resolution and help parties achieve resolution.

Management

The second factor, management, is rarely a problem for most judges. *Management* means giving a trial date at the appropriate time. If done too quickly (which is quite rare), the lawyers do not have adequate time to conduct discovery; prepare their clients for settlement; and watch for that magical window during which, in most cases, settlement is optimal. A psychologist acquaintance once told me that there is an average six-month gap between when one spouse wants a divorce and the other spouse accepts its inevitability. The six-month average is debatable, but there is no doubt that such a gap does exist in most cases. Scheduling a trial after both parties accept the inevitability of the divorce allows the agenda for negotiations to focus on the substantive issues, which lawyers are good at resolving, rather than the emotional ones (anger, hostility, recrimination, guilt), which lawyers can actually make worse.

However, courts do not always manage well. In certain cases, courts schedule trials too soon. In other, rare cases, courts refuse to even schedule a trial after sufficient time has elapsed. Certain parties are reluctant to "let go," whether to punish the other spouse or due to an inability to accept the inevitable. These are the cases in which a trial date is necessary to force the realities of negotiating to be recognized. Not uncommonly, then, all issues can be resolved except for relatively minor ones. A partial trial, which takes little time, can end the case while preserving precious court time and resources.

Although most judges promote resolution by settlement, most lawyers are in the best situation—notwithstanding the fact that not all lawyers are in tune with their own clients, cases, or even necessarily the concept of settlement—to advise the court when the time is ripe for a go-to-hell trial date (see chapter 7, "Positional Negotiation"). Of course, judges need to control their calendars. But, of everyone in a courtroom, judges have the least knowledge of the particulars, so in most cases they should rely on the lawyers for guidance.

Access

The third factor relating to judicial control of cooperation is access. The family law judge should be accessible to the bar, both informally and formally, and should provide sufficient leeway in access to the court.

For a number of years, I annually moderated a panel of family court judges for our local bar association. All of the judges were invited; and most, indeed, found time to appear. Although we had a formal agenda of issues or new cases to discuss, the real agenda was the opportunity for the practicing attorneys to mingle with the judges in a nonjudicial setting and have a venue for sharing ideas. The program was a sellout each year. I began each session by warning the lawyers that no question would be allowed that began with a phrase akin to "I have a case in which . . ." Rather, the goal was for a discussion of general topics and the judges' individual ideas on how to improve representation in their courts. Of course, there was a great deal of repetition: "Be prepared." "Be civil." "Try to settle before coming to court." These were routine suggestions. Yet, these sessions were highly valuable since the purpose was less the specifics of what each judge had to say than the concept of humanizing the judges by allowing lawyers to see them sans black robes.

Access also means providing sufficient court time and dates to allow cases to transition from the angry, revenge-laden stage to the acceptance stage. This includes scheduling pretrials and hearings at the convenience of the parties where possible. Each case moves at its own chosen speed. In most cases, the parties, not the court, should dictate the speed.

Conducting Pretrials

Some courts conduct pretrials on the record in open court. Worse, some courts do not conduct pretrials at all. The following is my strongest statement in this entire book: Failing to conduct a private pretrial with the attorneys is a derogation of a judge's duty.

The duty of a judge is to help resolve the cases assigned to that court. Sometimes that means trials. However, in the vast majority of cases, it means settlement. Courts do not promote settlement by holding pretrials on the record in open court—and they certainly don't promote settlement by not conducting pretrials at all. Judges need to meet privately with the lawyers, ask them to outline the issues, and then assess if and how they can be of assistance. Unless one (or both) of the parties is pro se, this meeting is far, far more effective in chambers where the attorneys do not have to posture for their clients.

Meeting with Clients

Some judges will take the parties into chambers following the pretrial or address them in open court. Either way, it is amazing the effect that a judge's comments can have on a party. The lawyers might have been preaching to the parties for months about the value of settlement, but when a judge says the same thing . . . well, it's different. A number of times in my career, I have heard a client quote a judge's advice to be peaceful—even though she has heard the same advice from me many, many times. The black robe makes a difference.

The speech does not have to be long or involved. It helps for a judge to reassure the parties that they have competent lawyers (hopefully that's the case!). But, it should go something like this:

> *My job is to decide any issues that you cannot agree upon with the assistance of your counsel. And if you need me to do so, I will, and I'll do the best that I can. However, you should be aware of several things: First, you and your attorneys know your situation better than I ever can, which makes it easier for you to customize a settlement. Second, I am restricted by the law regarding the type of decisions I can make, whereas you have far greater latitude to fashion something unique and creative if you wish. Finally, people who reach their own decisions generally find them easier to live with down the line than those who have decisions imposed upon them. So, I urge you, for your own best interests, to listen to your counsel, be flexible, and make some compromises to resolve these issues.*

Understanding Practicalities

Of course, some of these suggestions are not practical given the realities of modern-day court schedules. Judges need to be able to manage their caseloads, and there are sometimes other factors at play, like supervisory judges. Still, to the extent possible, judges should assist the settlement process by providing leadership, management, and access. While the parties and attorneys must respect the court, the courts should serve the people in promoting resolution.

Summary

Although attorneys are primarily responsible for conducting settlement negotiations, courts can help (or hinder!) the process. Through appropriate leadership, management, and access to the court, judges can help resolve these difficult cases.

Planned Early Negotiation 12

Please accept the following hypotheses, at least for the duration of this chapter:

- Most divorce cases are settled rather than litigated.
- Few cases involve the complexities of a Donald Trump divorce.
- At the beginning of a case, experienced lawyers generally have a pretty good idea of the range of likely results.
- The litigation process can be harmful to the relationship of the parties, which may scar their ability to coparent children in the future.
- If the parties could reach the same result on Day 1 that they could reach on Day 1,001, they should do so.

Such hypotheses make it easy to accept "planned early negotiation" (PEN), a concept explained by John Lande, law professor, in his book, *Lawyering with Planned Early Negotiation: How You Can Get Good Results for Clients and Make Money.*[1] The idea behind PEN is a simple one. If the likely end results can be recognized early on as falling within a narrow range, why not get there quickly?

Prison of Fear

Lande noted that although the use of PEN makes sense, many lawyers shy from using it:

> *In an all-too-common pattern in "litigation as usual," settlement comes only after the lawyers engage in adversarial posturing, the litigation process escalates the original conflict, the parties' relationship deteriorates, the process takes a long time and a lot of money, and none of the parties is particularly happy with the settlement. Although some lawyers enjoy this process and make a good living from it, many would prefer to use a more productive and efficient process, but they feel stuck in playing the adversarial "game."*[2]

Lande attributed much of the reluctance to engage in an early negotiations process to lawyers' fear: fear that a client will not retain them, fear that the case may be resolved before sufficient information is available, or other fears. He called this a "prison of fear."[3] To escape this prison of fear, Lande suggested, among other things, a careful case assessment, a planned exchange of information, "escape hatches," and appropriate compensation.[4]

Careful Case Assessment

The careful case assessment may be the most important facet of the process. After all, if you can choose the right cases for PEN—and avoid the wrong ones—at the beginning, the rest should be easy. According to Lande, a PEN process should be used only when it appears that

---

1. JOHN LANDE, LAWYERING WITH PLANNED EARLY NEGOTIATION: HOW YOU CAN GET GOOD RESULTS FOR CLIENTS AND MAKE MONEY 2 (Am. Bar Ass'n Section of Dispute Resolution 2011).
2. *Id.*
3. *Id.* at 5.
4. *Id.* at 10–17.

"everyone is willing to listen to others" and "take reasonable positions in negotiation."[5] After all, if extreme positional negotiating has to be involved, the "early" part of PEN will be lost.

Planned Exchange of Information

Similarly, the planned exchange of information is necessary for the "early" part of PEN to be accomplished. If extensive discovery is necessary, the time consumed will defeat the purpose. Therefore, a voluntary, open exchange of information is a necessary component.[6]

Escape Hatch

The escape hatch is an easy suggestion to accept. This process does not require anything to be approved by the court, unlike a collaborative divorce agreement. Therefore, if either party changes its mind and decides that early resolution is not in the best interests of that party, the process will resume a normal scheduling routine. Other than, perhaps, hurt feelings, nothing is lost.[7]

Appropriate Compensation

Appropriate compensation is a different matter. Most divorce lawyers charge strictly by the hour, which creates a potential conflict between the client's best interests and the lawyer's financial interest. Although most lawyers are highly professional, the fact remains that the longer the case drags on, the worse it is for the client. After all, hourly rates compensate lawyers solely for the time spent on the case. Therefore, unlike personal injury lawyers whose contingency agreements put the lawyer's financial interest in harmony with that of the client, divorce lawyers benefit by the exact opposite of the benefit to the client. However, since contingency fees are considered mostly unethical for family law attorneys, most attorneys feel that they have little choice but to charge by the hour.

Lande, noting the disparity between the lawyer's financial interest and the best interests of the client in shortening the process,[8] suggested

---

5. *Id.* at 11.
6. *Id.* at 12.
7. *Id.* at 14–15.
8. *Id.* at 16–17.

a variety of solutions.[9] It is not in the purview of this book to examine specific alternative billing strategies, but lawyers who seek to engage in PEN should explore some creative, nonhourly billing methods to avoid the lawyer-client financial conflict. Some ideas include offering a flat fee if the case settles and a higher rate if any portion of the case litigates, or offering a base rate and then a subjective bonus if the case settles early and both parties agree that such a bonus is warranted.

PEN: Positives and Negatives

PEN makes a great deal of sense. After all, if you needed surgery, would you prefer a lengthy, drawn-out process or one that resolves all issues quickly? Lawsuits, like surgery, should be handled as expeditiously and bloodlessly as possible. Thus, if a case can be settled early with the same results as it could be settled later, it is better for the clients to settle early. Of course, that is a big if.

There are several factors that conspire against PEN. One major factor that resonates in divorce cases and makes this concept questionable in many cases is, as mentioned frequently elsewhere in this book, the emotional levels inherent in family dissolution, which frequently prohibit getting to "yes" until the smoke has cleared. For example, one of the parties may still be resisting the very concept that the marriage is over; or one party may be bent on retaliation, or punishing the other spouse, for the divorce—or, worse yet, for misdeeds (perceived or real) during the marriage. Another factor is timing, a topic to which a whole chapter is devoted in this book (see chapter 3, "Timing"). Timing is everything when it comes to settlement: sometimes an early resolution is not possible due to the inability to get appraisals and other discovery completed quickly. In these cases, which may be the vast majority, PEN is simply not going to work.

Yet, for the right case, this technique is worth considering and keeping in an attorney's arsenal of available tools. It should be relatively easy to sell to clients, who are always interested in saving money. In the appropriate case, it is worth trying to sell the idea to opposing counsel as well.

---

9. *Id.* at 35–45.

Summary

Most experienced divorce lawyers can surmise the eventual resolution of a case very early in the process. In such a case, it may be worth proposing the PEN process as a means of minimizing the financial and emotion destruction of divorce on the parties.

Family Law–Specific Settlement Issues 13

Unlike most other areas of law, family law mixes sociology, psychology, child development, family dynamics, and numerous other areas of human interactions with the legal system. As a result, negotiations in family law have unique implications. This chapter will look at family law–specific issues and how these issues impact settlement negotiations.

Children

Perhaps the single most difficult issue in this field is the interests of children. After all, parenting issues are not generally legal issues. They are usually sociological issues such as child development; moral issues; or even religious issues. The law, using the well-meaning but vague term *best interests*, provides little guidance.

Custody and Visitation

It wasn't all that many years ago when it was relatively standard for Mom to get the kids and Dad to see them on alternate weekends and maybe one evening during the week. Now, not only are shared placement schedules common, but more and more frequently the kids are equally shared. Of course, in the olden days, wives stayed home and raised kids. Today, the mother is often working as much as the father, so why not share time with the children equally? Family law is simply keeping up with changing societal standards. You will need to talk to a futurist—or maybe a swami—to figure out where things are going in the future.

The important point to remember is that regardless of current trends, placement negotiation settlements should minimize conflict and keep in mind the best interests of the children.

Minimizing Conflict

In my state, children are appointed a guardian ad litem (GAL) when there is a significant dispute over custody or placement. When the child is over a certain age, usually at least three to five years old, the GAL will meet with the child to discuss the situation. When I first started serving as a GAL, I thought children would tell me that they wanted their parents to get back together. That rarely, if ever, happens. Instead, almost every child told me the same thing: "I want my parents to stop fighting."

This confirmed what I learned a number of years ago when I had the good fortune to be on the Special Concerns of Children Committee sponsored by the American Academy of Matrimonial Lawyers. One of the meetings featured a discussion with Dr. Judith Wallerstein, one of the leading researchers on the effects of divorce on children. According to Wallerstein, there are three major factors that determine the effects of divorce on children: (1) whether at least the primary home (better, both homes) offers a warm, caring, and loving environment; (2) the level of conflict between the parents; and (3) the individual psychological makeup of the child.

As lawyers, we can do nothing about the third factor—the DNA is what it is. We can help with the first factor by encouraging a client, when necessary, to be in therapy or take classes to improve their parenting skills. But it is the second factor on which we can have the most effect.

During settlement negotiations, lawyers should keep this second factor in mind. Obviously, in extreme cases where there are allegations of neglect or abuse, different rules apply. But, in many cases, the placement dispute is really one of arithmetic: X number of children plus two parents factored by seven days in the week. Mathematically, the placement problem can be solved in a number of different ways. However, the specifics of a placement schedule are less important than the general concept of resolution—in other words, get the parties to stop fighting.

Considering the Best Interests of Children

In a case in which I was involved, a forensic psychologist testified that she could not give an opinion to a reasonable degree of professional certainty regarding whether a particular placement schedule was in the best interests of the children. In a case with two reasonably adequate parents, she testified, the "best" placement schedule was to have no placement schedule at all—meaning an intact family. If that was impossible because the parents would not be living together, no placement schedule would be "best" for the children; she could only testify as to which schedule presented the "least detrimental alterative" for the children.

The concept of children's best interests is hardly a new one. King Solomon (circa 1000 B.C.E.) famously determined the real mother between two women both claiming the title by drawing his sword and threatening to cut the baby in half. The real mother was the woman who preferred to give up rather than harm the child. How nice settlement negotiations would be if people truly behaved that way three thousand years later!

It is far easier to lecture (or, as a colleague of mine puts it, to sermonize) about putting the children first than to practice doing so. Lawyers should develop strategies to make sure that they consider the best interests of the children, including keeping in mind and reminding their clients that in many cases fighting causes more harm to the children than any particular placement or visitation schedule. And since many placement issues are not really legal matters but rather child development matters, the issues can often be resolved in mediation by professionals trained in that area, such as social workers, psychotherapists, or psychologists.

Placement versus Child Support

Placement issues can frequently get sucked into monetary considerations because in many states, the more time the payer (usually, but not always, the father) spends with the child, the less child support he will pay. This factor is complicated by the mistrust inherent in divorce and custody proceedings. Consider the following situation: A father who allowed his wife to assume most (or all) child-rearing tasks while the marriage was intact now seeks a great amount of time with his children. This desire may very well be a legitimate wish to spend more time with the children. On the other hand, the father's desire may not be for such positive reasons. It may be a threat to punish his wife or a calculated way to pay less money for support. Even if the father's desire is for legitimate reasons, the wife who has rarely (or never) seen her husband undertake such a role may not believe the request to be genuine.

A lawyer can test the sincerity of the client by asking a simple question. If the wife is suspicious that her husband (your client, in this example) is less interested in time with the children than he is in not paying support, ask the husband what is more important to him: money or his children. The correct answer, of course, is the children.

On occasion when I have tried this technique, I cannot get my client to give me that answer. Rather, he argues that the two are inseparable and that he cannot afford to be a father while paying child support. Of course, that's not true, and the very failure to give the correct response is answer enough.

But when your client does give the correct answer, then ask for permission to take the issue of child support off the table (discussed in more detail in chapter 17, "Creative Settlement Techniques"). In other words, ask for authority to make the following settlement proposal:

My client believes that your client's reluctance to agree to the expanded placement is due to her belief that he is only interested in paying less child support rather than being an involved father. In order to prove to you that is not true, he has authorized me to tell you that he will pay the maximum amount of child support under our state guidelines regardless of the eventual placement schedule. Child support is thus off the table as a negotiating item. Knowing that, can we discuss what placement would be in the best interests of the children?

The same approach may work in other scenarios as well, such as when the mother is accused of using the children as meal tickets. Removing a related issue from the agenda can ease mistrust and promote resolution.

Support

Incentive to Work

A client of mine whose business was negotiating with labor unions compared support issues to worker-company issues. The more the company pays the workers, the less competitive the company becomes, jeopardizing future revenue. The less the company pays, the less incentive the employees have to be loyal to the company. And an inability to compromise would result in a strike, which would be a loss for both sides.

Similarly, in family law, the more support paid, the less incentive to create income. Granted, most payers recognize the need to support their children and their ex-spouse. However, in cases involving employees who have some control over their income, such as those paid on a commission basis, the result is not always the maximization of income. After all, people tend to work harder and longer and make more money if they get to control more of their income and keep more of their money for themselves (duh!). We are a capitalistic society.

Of course, employment decisions, even independent of family dynamics and divorce emotions, are not always purely economic. The most common example is the mother (and, increasingly commonly, the father) who leaves the job market so she can stay home with the children. In many cases, even factoring in the costs of child care, the family would financially profit if she worked outside the home. Yet, some parents choose to make the economically less attractive choice because they prefer a parent to be at home with the children. Similarly, employees change jobs—or sometimes simply leave jobs—due to working conditions, relationships with coworkers or their boss, the type of work, possibilities of advancement, or a myriad of other reasons not financially advantageous. In an intact family, as long as no government assistance is needed, such a decision is no one else's business. Not so, however, when the parties are no longer aligned in interest.

The concept of "shirking"—or a party intentionally working for less money or for no money at all—is impossible to adjudicate on a subjective scale. Courts do not have the power to read minds and are thus incapable of deciding whether the employment choice was made to deprive the other spouse of support or for another, less nefarious reason. Since it is nearly impossible in many cases to ferret out the reason for employment choices, courts tend to focus solely on the objective factor of maximizing income.

Thus, lawyers need to find mechanisms in settlement to maximize this incentive. The concept is to give the working spouse an incentive to create income while providing an advantage to the other spouse. One means of doing this is to "divert" some support into a college fund for children or simply into a designated account to be used for specific child-related purposes, such as summer camp, a car, a school trip, or any of the myriad "special" costs that children incur.

In settlement, lawyers need to be thinking of incentives to both parties. By paying money directly to children (either for now or later), the payer has an incentive to perform the extra work often required to generate that income. At the same time, since the money benefits the children, the other party has an incentive to negotiate so that the earner will, well, earn!

Face-Saving

During World War II, President Franklin D. Roosevelt made it clear that the only peace agreement acceptable to the allies would be the unconditional surrender of the enemy. Indeed, when late in the war some German officers sought a peace agreement, Roosevelt refused to even consider it. As a result, after Hiroshima and Nagasaki, the Japanese did not even seek a compromise, knowing one was not available.

Divorce, however, is not warfare (although, unfortunately, there are similarities on occasion). In *Getting to YES: Negotiating Agreement Without Giving In*, Roger Fisher and William Ury discussed the concept of "face-saving," which they defined as "a person's need to reconcile the stand he takes in a negotiation or an agreement with his principles and with his past words and deeds."[1] Allowing the other side to save face is more important in a family law context than in most, if not all, negotiation areas, especially if there will be an ongoing relationship between the parties, either through children or through support.

Once, I represented a very successful general contractor who told me that the secret of his success was that he would not engage a subcontractor who underbid the job. My first question was, "Why would a subcontractor underbid a job?" He explained that sometimes a

---

1. ROGER FISHER & WILLIAM URY, GETTING TO YES: NEGOTIATING AGREEMENT WITHOUT GIVING IN 28 (1981).

subcontractor did so to secure future business, other times to just stay busy, and sometimes because they did not appreciate the true cost. My second question was, "Why is that bad for you—after all, wouldn't you make a higher profit based on the low bid?" His response was yes, but only in the short term. In the long term, he said, a new, profitable job would become available, and the subcontractor would turn all of his attentions and time to that job and ignore his. Alternatively, the subcontractor would simply realize that he was losing money on the job. All in all, my client refused to deal with a subcontractor who did not make a profit because the work would not be adequately performed—if it was performed at all.

In family law, this is a matter of perception. My late partner, Leonard Loeb, used to say that the best result for a support recipient was to negotiate the maximum amount of support that allowed the payer to think that he won. If the payer feels that he lost, like the subcontractor who underbid the job, there is no incentive for him to continue to work into the future and create income. At the earliest point possible—a slight downturn in the economy, the earliest possible retirement age—he will seek some means to get out from under his burden. In extreme cases, this can even mean missing payments and becoming a scofflaw.

To avoid this result, a family law attorney should never demand unconditional surrender. In any negotiations, some concession, even a minor one, should be given at the end as a "closer." Simply put, it is not sufficient to reach a great settlement on paper unless the paper turns out to be negotiable currency. (It is important, of course, that the client be educated about why saving face is important so that he can understand the reason for any concessions.)

Summary

There are certain issues that are specific to family law and therefore require unique settlement strategies. These issues include custody/visitation and support.

Fighting over variations in child placement or visitation can harm children more than the specifics of any particular schedule. Lawyers need to encourage clients to negotiate for the long-term interests of their children.

Support also merits special considerations in family law as there are long-term consequences regarding the incentive to generate income.

Lawyers should try to devise some creative means to incentivize the payer to create income. Due to the ongoing relationship between the parties following the legal action, however, lawyers should never push for the last dollar. Letting the opposing party save face by allowing last-minute compromises, rather than making ultimatums and demanding unconditional surrender, can lead to better relations between the parties in the future.

Mediation 14

One of the most remarkable phenomena in family law in recent years has been the widespread use of mediation. Mediation is a dispute resolution process in which a neutral third person who has no power to impose a decision helps the parties reach an agreement. Once unheard of in family law cases, it is now mandatory in many states and widely used on a voluntary basis.

Reasons for the Success of Mediation

Mediation became an essential part of resolving family law matters for one simple reason: it frequently works where other settlement efforts have failed. Mediation can be successful for several reasons.

First, a third party can sometimes break an impasse that has caused negotiations to come to a halt. When the parties are both strong willed and unwilling to budge on various issues, a mediator can open up lines of communication that may have closed during adversarial negotiations. Put another way, where inertia has caused negotiations to come to a stop, a mediator can get things moving again.

Second, mediation injects a fresh and unbiased viewpoint into the negotiations. Lawyers sometimes get so close to their clients' objectives that they fail to see the forest for the trees. It can be beneficial to hear a neutral, independent, trusted professional's opinion and insight because it can bring the parties back to reality. Due to an inherent objectivity, the mediator may be able to see solutions that the parties do not see because the mediator is not emotionally invested in the outcome.

Third, in many family law cases, children are involved, and the issues are not legal at all but emotional. In such cases, a trained mediator who is also a mental health professional can turn the mediation session into a therapeutic one. Such therapy may be extremely valuable to quell the emotions and allow practicality and rationality to prevail.

Finally, mediation is successful because it is a confidential process. There is no court reporter taking down every word said about and between the parties. Some mediators, in fact, shred any notes taken after the case is closed. The parties do not have to worry about their "dirty laundry" being aired in public. It gives many people comfort to know that mediation is not public like a court hearing. Parties can talk more freely regarding private issues without various people in a courtroom listening to their every word.

Pitfalls of Mediation

As valuable as mediation can be in many cases, it is no panacea. After all, if the mediator's goal is to settle a case, an imbalanced settlement is within the definition of success even though the long-term implications may be seriously troubling. This is not consistent with the goal of the attorneys representing the parties. Their goal is not simply any settlement but rather a settlement within the range of reasonable results for the client. To achieve this type of result, the lawyer representing a party has to be alert to the following dangers of mediation: mediators with limited skill and experience, mediation with unrepresented parties and a significant disparity in power, and facilitative mediation with represented parties.

Mediators with Limited Skill and Experience

A mediator's goal is to help parties come to an agreement, but sometimes the issues are beyond the skills and training of the mediator. A mediator should not be giving legal advice to either party. However, although many of the issues discussed in mediation in family law are nonlegal, legal issues will arise. The parties should expect the mediator to know enough substantive law in order to guide them in coming to an agreement. Mediators who do not know sufficient law about a specific issue may have a hard time understanding why a party refuses to budge. If the issues are financial, using a mediator not versed in taxes or valuation issues may confuse matters. If the parties do not understand the legal implications of an agreement, are they making an informed decision when deciding to sign it?

This problem can be avoided by careful selection of a mediator. The parties already know what topics and issues need to be addressed. Therefore, they should seek a mediator who has experience and/or training with these issues.

Mediation with Unrepresented Parties and a Significant Disparity in Power

Mediation is often conducted without attorneys present. If clients are not strong negotiators or do not articulate arguments as well as their counterparts, they will be at a disadvantage. If, as is common, there is a power or knowledge imbalance between the parties, the results may not be equitable. After all, the reason that many people hire an attorney is because they seek a lawyer's skill at negotiation and bargaining.

The goal of a mediator is simply to achieve a settlement, so a power or knowledge imbalance may not be an impediment to "success" as defined by the mediator. If the settlement is a victory for one party and a disaster for the other, the mediator still did his job, which was to settle the case. This danger can be avoided if both parties have lawyers representing them during the mediation. In order to keep the mediation reflective of the parties' and not the lawyers' words, the mediator could ask the lawyers not to speak during the mediation proceedings but could allow parties the opportunity to take breaks to speak with their attorneys. This would allow weaker parties access to a source of information to help them feel educated about the issues and thus empowered.

Facilitative Mediation with Represented Parties

Facilitative mediation is akin to playing ping-pong. The ball bounces back and forth, sometimes with more force and sometimes spinning or curving. However, if the two attorneys cannot bounce the ball back and forth between themselves without the help of a mediator, they are not serving their clients' interests. Lawyers, at least in the field of family law, should not need a third person to relay proposals. Therefore, facilitative mediation would be a waste of resources. On the other hand, evaluative mediation, where the mediator's role is expanded to include critiquing proposals and making suggestions, can be invaluable.

Selection of a Mediator

Selecting the Type of Mediator

Mediators tend to come in several varieties, and the choice should depend on the nature of the issues involved. The varieties include mental health professionals, retired judges, and respected lawyers.

Mental health professionals such as social workers or psychologists are one type of mediator. Such professionals often mediate cases involving child-related issues, which is appropriate as the issues are usually less legal and more child development related. For example, a case may involve whether a child's development is helped or hindered by a particular placement schedule—a subject that is not addressed in law schools but that may be at the heart of the dispute. Certain nonlegal professionals may have received training in this very area, which will likely make them excellent mediators.

Retired judges are another common type of mediator. These judges bring the advantage of being able to say, "While I can't tell you how the judge in this case would rule on this issue, I can tell you how I used to rule on it when I was on the bench." Often, settlement in a case is promoted by knowing the likely outcome of a contested trial, which is the basis of a BATNA, so this type of experience can be invaluable.

Respected (usually meaning older) lawyers are yet another type of mediator. These lawyers usually have an advantage, as mediators, over retired judges because respected lawyers have actually represented divorce clients before. This often means that they have insight into the emotional issues that often overwhelm the legal ones. Unlike former judges (unless they practiced law before assuming the bench), respected lawyers have had experience convincing clients to compromise. On the other hand, respected lawyers cannot bring down the authoritative hammer of "This is the way I would rule if I were the judge."

One caveat: nonlawyers mediating financial issues. Some of these mediators may be practicing law without a license. Although they may have training as mediators, their lack of experience in this field (their own divorce does not count) should cause hesitation before hiring such people for divorce mediation proceedings.

Selecting the Particular Mediator

In any event, it is more important that the parties agree to the particular mediator than anything else. After all, the purpose of the mediator is to get the parties to agree. In evaluative mediation, the mediator will be commenting on the proposals and perhaps making one of his own. If the other side does not "buy into" that particular mediator, the chances of negotiating a mediated settlement diminish. And there is no point to mediation other than reaching a settlement.

So, start the discussion. After deciding on the variety of mediator that is preferred, the lawyers should consider particular individuals. If the same name does not occur to both lawyers, one should prepare a list of three to five acceptable mediators and the other should pick from the list. Or, better yet, both sides should prepare such a list and then compare for overlapping names.

If you don't have prior experience with the particular mediator being considered, do some research. Most mediators will be pleased to give references from successful mediations. Call one or more of the lawyers involved. Ask about the mediator's style. Is it truly evaluative? Does the mediator test the parties' positions? Will the mediator come up with his own proposals? Is the mediator proactive or passive? As with many other things in life, being forewarned is being forearmed.

Preparation for Mediation

Mediation requires as much, if not more, preparation than any settlement conference. In addition to discussion with a client about opening, optimal, and go-to-hell positions, a lawyer needs to discuss the concept and process of mediation with the client. The client needs to understand, for example, that in an evaluative mediation, the mediator will express opinions but not dictate a result.

Some cases require more than one mediation session. For those, there should be a debriefing after the first session and a preparation meeting before the second.

Postsettlement

Congratulations! You have reached an agreement through mediation!

Before celebrating—in fact, before the agreement is even written—have one more meeting with your client and make sure that you both understand the same settlement.

Ideally, immediately after an agreement is reached, the mediator will draft a settlement agreement or memorandum. Occasionally, there is not sufficient time to draft the document immediately. However, sometimes people hear different things, perhaps because they are only hearing what they want to hear, so the agreement should be reduced to writing as soon as possible.

Summary

Mediation can be a highly effective way of settling a case. However, a lawyer has a number of roles to perform to make sure that mediation is successful. These include selecting the type of mediator as well as the particular mediator; preparing the client for the mediation; and participating in the mediation, in certain cases as both an advocate for the client and an advocate for settlement (and, no, these roles are not inconsistent).

Collaborative Divorce[1]

Within the past ten years, a settlement process known as "collaborative divorce" has exploded across the country. Begun in Minnesota and then spreading to California, it now has thousands of adherents all over the country—and even around the world.[2]

Collaborative divorce is a settlement-based process in which both parties and their attorneys commit to resolving all issues without recourse to the courts. The process includes four-way meetings, voluntary disclosure of all economic interests with no formal discovery, and joint appraisals of assets where necessary. Unlike mediation, both parties must have attorneys, which eliminates the potential power imbalance of mediation. In many cases, the process is multidisciplinary and includes mental health therapists as well as neutral financial experts trained in the

---

1. Portions of this chapter were previously published in part in other sources written by Gregg Herman.
2. "The International Academy of Collaborative Professionals (IACP) has 4,200 members in 24 countries and [lists] more than 300 Collaborative practice groups." John Lande, *An Empirical Analysis of Collaborative Practice*, 49 FAM. COURT REV. 257, 257 (Apr. 2011).

collaborative process. When minor children are involved, there may be a neutral child specialist.[3]

The essential part of the process is an enforceable agreement calling for both attorneys to withdraw and transfer the case to litigation counsel if the process fails and litigation ensues.[4] It is this enormous threat of withdrawal that serves as an impetus for the lawyers and the parties to engage in creative problem solving rather than threatening to go, or actually going, to court. The goal is to make the cost of failure to everyone so extreme that settlement becomes almost imperative. Collaborative divorce is designed to completely remove litigation—and even the threat of litigation—from the settlement process. There is, quite simply, no day of trial in a collaborative divorce. Thus, collaborative divorce avoids wasted resources because the financial costs of trial preparation are completely eliminated. Just as importantly, the sword-wielding threat of going to trial is eliminated. The result is to lessen (if not eliminate) the bitter taste of the adversarial legal process that may tarnish future relations between the litigants and impair the parties' ability to coparent in the future. As mediation specialist Yishai Boyarin noted, although most cases settle before trial, "the quality of the process and settlement achieved under the shadow of litigation is different than those achieved without such a threat."[5]

Attorney Pauline Tesler, a leading collaborative law advocate, described collaborative law as a method that "combines the explicit commitment to settlement that is at the core of mediation with the enhanced creative power of a model that builds legal advocacy and counsel into the settlement process from the start, as well as conflict management and guidance in negotiations."[6] In addition to a beneficial effect on clients, collaborative law may have a dramatic effect on lawyers as well:

---

3. Gregg Herman, *Collaborative Divorce*, 15 AM. J. FAM. L. 249, 249–50 (2001).
4. *Id.*
5. Yishai Boyarin, *Generating Win-Win Results: Negotiating Conflicts in the Drafting Process of the Uniform Collaborative Law Act*, 38 HOFSTRA L. REV. 495, 504 (2009).
6. PAULINE H. TESLER, COLLABORATIVE LAW: ACHIEVING EFFECTIVE RESOLUTION IN DIVORCE WITHOUT LITIGATION 4 (ABA Section of Family Law 2001).

With experience, collaborative lawyers learn to behave in ways that significantly enhance their clients' ability to achieve their stated goals of amicable settlement. These behaviors differ dramatically from how lawyers learn to represent clients in law school and from how they behave in conventional litigation practice. Effective collaborative lawyers cultivate thought processes, attitudes, and skills entirely different from the armaments of a trial lawyer. Many collaborative lawyers report that as they embark upon learning this new craft, their understanding of the dynamics of divorce and the appropriate role of lawyers in the divorce process undergoes profound shifts.[7]

In fact, collaborative lawyers talk about undergoing a "paradigm shift" or "retooling" their approach to practicing law.[8]

Agreement to Proceed

The collaborative divorce process starts with a lawyer making a determination that a certain case would be right for the process. The process should not be used in any cases where there are allegations of hidden assets or income. For the most part, it should not be used in cases where there is mental illness or spousal abuse or substance abuse, unless the abuser and the abusee are fully cooperating with mental health therapy.

If the case seems appropriate for a collaborative divorce approach, it requires the agreement of the client's spouse and that spouse's lawyer. The process cannot work without each party having collaborative lawyers because such a case would lack the leverage of the mutual, mandatory withdrawal, which is basic to the collaborative divorce model.

If both parties and both lawyers agree, an agreement is signed by all to have the case treated under collaborative divorce principles. In a collaborative divorce, as mentioned above, there is no formal discovery. Both sides must agree to make full and voluntary disclosure. All appraisals are joint. Both attorneys will refrain from attack letters and confrontational behavior.

---

7. *Id.*
8. *Id.* at 27–28.

The Disqualification Agreement

What sets collaborative law apart from other settlement models is the disqualification agreement—the revolutionary concept that a lawyer is being hired in lawsuit for every reason *except* to actually represent the client in court. This agreement makes collaborative divorce unique.

The disqualification agreement is necessary to the process due to the inherent costs of failure. First, for the parties, it costs significant money to start over with new counsel. Second, for the lawyers, failure means not only losing fees but losing the client as well. There is a huge incentive to settle because the costs of failure are significant for both the client and the lawyer.

The Role of the Mental Health Professional

In some collaborative divorce models, both parties must have a trained mental health therapist coach them through the divorce. Other models do not make therapists mandatory, just recommended.

The similarity between collaborative divorce and cooperative divorce (discussed in chapter 16, "Cooperative Divorce") in the utilization of mental health "coaches" is telling. Both recognize the importance of lawyers operating within the sphere of their profession. When parties are not in counseling, they tend to use their lawyers as mental health therapists, a role for which many lawyers are ill suited. Too, mental health therapists serve as a "911" number for people going through a divorce. Absent such therapy, some people may let their emotions rule their intellect, making the attorney's role all the more difficult. Although the same is true in any divorce, in both collaborative and cooperative divorce, the importance of a client maintaining emotional stability is critical as both processes are dedicated toward resolution.

The Role of the Financial Professional

The financial professional's role in collaborative divorce is designed to assist the parties in reaching resolution. Therefore, the parties commit to utilizing appraisers on a bilateral basis only—no unilateral appraisals are allowed. Some collaborative divorce models utilize a financial specialist as a neutral to help gather financial information and recommend tax-effective settlements.

Although this is similar to the role of the financial professional in cooperative divorce, there remains a significant difference. In collaborative divorce, part of the "penalty" for not reaching a settlement is the disqualification of the financial expert if the case goes to trial. The resultant cost of starting over with new appraisers serves as an incentive for the parties to make the sort of compromises necessary to reach a settlement.

The Role of the Judge

In a collaborative divorce, the role of the judge is minimal. In some models, the judge can do some informal mediation in a pretrial. For the most part, however, the primary principle of collaborative divorce is to avoid court. Although there is a world of difference between a pretrial with a judge and a contested hearing, most collaborative models minimize the involvement of the judge, if not avoid it altogether. Unlike cooperative divorce, collaborative divorce likes to avoid even the use of the words *court* and *judge*, to the extent possible.

Downsides of Collaborative Divorce

No system is perfect, of course, and collaborative divorce has certain negatives. These need to be weighed against the positive attributes of removing even the threat of litigation from the process.

Risks of the Disqualification Requirement

The disqualification requirement may not work when there has been domestic violence, mental illness, or substance abuse, even when mental health therapists are utilized. Most collaborative practitioners will not sign a disqualification agreement in these types of cases unless appropriate counseling, be it anger management or alcohol counseling, is part of the agreement. Yet, as every practitioner knows, recidivism rates for these issues are relatively high. Given the costs of disqualification, some practitioners will not sign disqualification agreements at all when these issues are involved. Once, in a presentation on collaborative law, I mentioned that collaborative divorce may be precluded when these issues are involved; one judge exclaimed, "That eliminates 90 percent of my caseload!" Although that may be an exaggeration (or perhaps not!), it does limit the number of available cases for this process.

The threat of disqualification has other risks, too. In some cases, it can be used to try to exact a better settlement; in other cases, the lack of a credible trial threat can cause the matter to be prolonged at considerable emotional and financial cost.

Costs

Not surprisingly, collaborative divorce can be expensive. The costs of the ancillary professionals, such as mental health therapists (who typically would not be covered by insurance), a child specialist, and a financial neutral may substantially increase the costs of the action. This is ironic as many of the people seeking collaborative divorce seem to be doing so in order to save the costs of litigation. Indeed, studies of the process have found that its clients tend to be "white, middle-aged, well educated and affluent,"[9] and other studies have noted "'mixed findings' about whether parties saved . . . money" by utilizing the collaborative process versus what they would have spent in a traditional divorce.[10]

Settlement Rates

Although there are few studies of collaborative divorce, the research shows that settlement rates are similar to a traditional negotiation process.[11] Given the additional risks of a collaborative case, it seems reasonable to expect a higher probability of settling, but that does not appear to be the case.

Incompatibility of Clients/Lawyers with Method

Collaborative divorce requires attorneys and clients who can, for lack of a better phrase, collaborate with each other.

In order for the process to be successful, two things need to be true. First, the lawyers must choose appropriate clients. Second, the lawyers must be trained in the collaborative process and practice accordingly.

Collaborative divorce is not right for every client. If one client is seeking to use the process to gain an advantage or manipulate the other client, the process is doomed. Yet, studies have shown that many lawyers do not "screen cases for appropriateness." Until recently, "there

---

9. Lande, *supra* note 2, at 260.
10. *Id.* at 270.
11. *Id.*

was no screening protocol [whatsoever] for domestic violence" cases.[12] Currently, several states have enacted the Uniform Collaborative Law Act, which includes a screening requirement; nevertheless, the majority of states have yet to follow suit.[13] Boyarin observed thus:

> *Indeed, a strong concern exists as to whether a party with a history of domestic violence can meaningfully participate, or may even be harmed by participating, in an interests-based negotiation process that places her face-to-face with the perpetrator of the violence in a setting that requires compromise and rational thinking. This type of concern would be exacerbated where the domestic violence victim is expected, and perhaps compelled by her lawyer, to act and make decisions based on her "highest acting self."*[14]

Boyarin noted that a screening process is beneficial because "clients with a history of domestic violence will be drawn to [collaborative law] based on [collaborative law]'s reputation as an innovative process that safeguards their particular needs."[15]

Not only must the client be right for collaborative law, but the lawyer must be a good fit, too. Although some collaborative law groups screen prospective members and only admit those whose style of practice fits with the settlement-based model, others are open to any lawyer who sat—or even slept—through the requisite training. The result may be lawyers who have the training but neither the skills nor the temperament to practice collaboratively, which is inconsistent with the goals of a truly collaborative divorce. John Lande, law professor and mediator, noted that "[f]or some lawyers, there [i]s a 'quasi-evangelical quality' to [collaborative practice] that 'border[s] on an ideological commitment.'"[16] Whether that quality is conducive to the type of process involved in a collaborative divorce case is questionable.

---

12. *Id.* at 267.
13. Uniform Collaborative Law Act (approved July 15, 2009). As of July 31, 2012, four states and the District of Columbia had enacted the act, and three other states were considering it. Press Release, Uniform Law Comm'n, Hawaii Enacts the Uniform Collaborative Law Act (July 31, 2012).
14. Boyarin, *supra* note 5, at 531.
15. *Id.* at 535.
16. Lande, *supra* note 2, at 262.

Summary

Collaborative divorce is not for every case—or even for every lawyer. In fact, given the attention and publicity that it receives in both the general and the legal media, it has affected only a very small percentage of cases due in large part to its costs and its risks. Still, there are a certain number of cases for which it may be the best strategy to employ; so all family law attorneys should have enough familiarity with collaborative divorce to be able, first, to assess which cases are right for it and, second, to appropriately use it.

Cooperative Divorce[1]   16

Although collaborative divorce has proven highly successful in certain cases, it is not appropriate for certain cases and a disaster in others. Another concept, cooperative divorce, may, in some of these cases, be a valuable settlement-based alternative to collaborative divorce.

Collaborative Divorce: An Overview

Collaborative divorce, as discussed in the previous chapter, is a settlement-based process in which both parties and their attorneys commit to resolving all issues; the key aspect of this method is an enforceable agreement calling for both attorneys to withdraw and transfer the case to litigation counsel if the process fails and litigation ensues.[2]

In my experience, the process works very well in many cases. By eliminating court dates, the collaborative process can avoid the inefficiency and pressure of trial preparation; adjournments; and last-minute, courthouse-step settlements. More important, collaborative divorce

---

1. Portions of this chapter were previously published in Gregg Herman, *Cooperative Divorce*, 19 Am. J. Fam. L. 161 (Fall 2005).
2. *See* Gregg Herman, *Collaborative Divorce*, 15 Am. J. Fam. L. 249 (2001).

can minimize the emotional costs for the parties. When the collaborative process fails, however, a financial and emotional disaster occurs, often making the result worse than if the process had never been initiated.

It comes as no surprise that there are many cases for which collaborative divorce is not appropriate.[3] In order for the process to work, there needs to be a certain amount of trust, communication, and cooperation between the parties: trust because there will be no formal discovery, and the process should not be used to disqualify a lawyer; communication because the process entails four-way meetings and absent a sufficient degree of listening and appropriate responding, these meetings can be disastrous; and cooperation for the same reasons as the first two. The problem, of course, is that if a couple has a significant amount of trust, communication, and cooperation, they wouldn't be getting divorced in the first place. Thus, collaborative divorce has to find those cases where these factors are sufficiently impaired to cause the marriage to fail but not so much as to prohibit the process from working. Where the process is not appropriate or fails to work, the only other option in most jurisdictions is the standard divorce scenario with all of its attendant horrors.

Cooperative Divorce: An Overview

Cooperative divorce, however, may be a viable option where the parties want a settlement-based approach yet do not cooperate, communicate, or trust each other enough to sign an agreement that would disqualify their lawyers if it failed.[4]

---

3. My office studied divorce filings in an adjacent county over a three-year period. We discovered that only approximately 1.4 percent of divorce cases filed a collaborative stipulation in each of the years studied; and, despite a well-publicized process by a collaborative group with strong leadership, the number of collaborative stipulations has not been increasing much during the period studied. I am aware of no other such studies anywhere else in the country. Gregg Herman, *Family Law: Why Are There Fewer Collaborative Divorce Filings?*, WIS. L.J. (June 8, 2011), *available at* http://wislawjournal.com/2011/06/08/why-are-there-fewer-collaborative-divorce-filings/.
4. John Lande & Gregg Herman, *Fitting the Forum to the Family Fuss*, 42 FAM. CT. REV. 280 (2004).

As with collaborative divorce, in a cooperative divorce the parties agree to work toward a settlement, voluntarily disclose all financial interests, refrain from formal discovery, and use joint appraisals of assets. Unlike collaborative divorce, however—and this is a significant difference—a cooperative divorce agreement is a statement of intent only and is not binding on the parties.

What is the purpose of a cooperative divorce agreement if it carries no teeth? First, the nonbinding promise to cooperate and work toward settlement helps to dissipate at least some of the mistrust and suspicion that can cause unnecessary financial and emotional costs in a divorce. Second, by eliminating the disqualification feature, cooperative divorce eliminates the possibility of a party manipulating the process. Finally, cooperative divorce allows the threat of litigation, which is necessary in certain cases to keep the process on track and negotiations honest.

Cooperative divorce, being a problem-solving approach, may require some or all of the following understandings:

- The divorce process should not be used for emotional relief.
- The problem-solving approach should be emphasized as opposed to a confrontation or litigation approach.
- Children are not to be used as pawns. Their best interests must be considered, which normally means regular, frequent contact with both parents.
- Complete and accurate financial disclosure should be promptly compiled and provided, as well as supplementary information upon changes occurring during the process.
- Any action that will result in antagonizing the other side or engendering distrust should be avoided. Each side should treat the other side as it would want to be treated. For example, attorneys should avoid the type of written communication that merely articulates the client's grievance or position, which usually results in a countercommunication and increasing ill will between the parties.
- Lawyers and the parties should treat the other side with courtesy, trying to overlook actions that appear to be or are, in fact, uncooperative or insulting.
- If resolution of all differences does not occur between the attorneys, a third-party mediator should be employed. The last resort is to submit the dispute to the court.

- Early mediation should be considered for procedural and substantive issues, which may assist in resolving temporary issues that are otherwise unresolvable.

The Role of the Mental Health Professional

As with collaborative divorce, there may be a role for the mental health professional in a cooperative divorce as a "coach" rather than as a therapist. A therapist will attempt to diagnose any underlying abnormalities and develop a treatment plan to either cure or at least cope with them. A coach is merely trying to get the person through the process; the treatment is deferred until later.

The difference is significant. During a divorce, much as in warfare, there is little time for dispassionate reflection while bullets are whirring overhead. The involvement of a mental health professional may be critical to get the person through the battle psychologically unscathed. After the divorce, the mental health professional may be in a better position to diagnose and recommend treatment as need be for any underlying condition.

The Role of the Financial Professional

Again, as with a collaborative divorce, there is a role for a neutral financial professional in a cooperative divorce. The financial professional is normally a certified public accountant. It is helpful for the financial professional to be a trained mediator in order to understand and employ mediation concepts and techniques. The different roles of the financial professional in the cooperation model may be as a mediator, a court-appointed neutral financial expert, or a jointly retained neutral financial expert.

The mediator role may be the most problematic because few financial professionals receive training in dispute resolution. However, as either a court-appointed or jointly retained neutral expert, the financial professional usually reaps significant savings for the parties. The smaller savings is, of course, the fact that the costs of the expert are shared. The greater savings is attorney fees because the lawyers won't need to analyze two appraisal reports and then argue about which one should prevail. In addition, if the expert is court appointed, there will be little doubt about the court's finding on the issue, which, again, represents a significant savings in attorney fees.

The Role of the Judge

The most significant professional person involved in the cooperation model can be the judge. The judge's role in the cooperative process is to limit the parties' involvement with the court by facilitating settlement at the earliest possible time with the best chance of a lasting solution in the most cases possible.

The family law judge should learn the principles of mediation and apply those principles whenever possible at hearings, informal conferences, and management conferences. The judge should be accessible to the bar, both informally and formally. Communication of the judge's policy is important so that ideas can be shared and tested in order to create an atmosphere of cooperative partnership with the bar in planning for the efficient processing of the family law caseload.

Why Bother with a Cooperative Agreement?

The most frequent question that lawyers ask about cooperative divorce is "Why bother? After all, aren't most cases handled in a cooperative manner?" (That's actually two questions, but never mind!)

The answer to the second question is yes. As all divorce lawyers know, the vast majority of cases not only settle, but they do so professionally and, well, frequently cooperatively.

Please note, however, that this fact refers to what divorce lawyers know. The general public does not know this. Most people are highly distrustful of lawyers in general and divorce lawyers specifically. Whether this is a result of media portrayal, advertising by lawyers, or the rare instances in which lawyers act unprofessionally, this perception must be taken into account. Few parties knew a divorce lawyer before needing one, and many never hired any lawyer in the past.

It is to reassure these clients that cooperative divorce has its greatest value. The agreement does not take long to prepare or execute. It has no downsides, as does a collaborative agreement, as it cannot be cited in court and trial remains an option. The few minutes that it takes to prepare and execute such an agreement helps to reassure skeptical clients that reality differs from their perception of divorce lawyers as nail-eating, incendiary gladiators.

A collaborative lawyer once told me that lawyers need to emulate doctors in having multiple tools available. In assessing a cardiac patient, for example, absent an emergency situation, a cardiologist will consider various options, such as lifestyle changes, medication, minor invasive surgery, and full open-heart surgery. Why then, she queried in discussing the potential value of collaborative divorce, do family law attorneys only offer the options of trial versus traditional, positional settlement negotiation?

Her reasoning is a good argument for the availability of collaborative divorce for the proper case. But why stop there? There are many cases (some might argue, in fact, most cases) in which the disqualification agreement, which is critical to collaborative practice, is not appropriate, but a less drastic settlement process would be helpful. Many of the advantages of collaborative practice, such as the neutral professional, the mental health coach, and, most important, the degree of assurance to the parties, can be utilized in a cooperative case without the substantial risks of the disqualification agreement. And there is no downside. No one would ever question the ethical propriety of acting cooperatively. After all, unlike in a collaborative case, if the cooperative process does not succeed, there is a Plan B available that is not a disaster for all involved.

It is puzzling why cooperative law is not more common. Perhaps it is because it does not spark the evangelic fervor that energizes many in the collaborative movement. Perhaps it is because lawyers have not considered the value of simply reassuring clients of their intent to behave cooperatively. In any event, a process with no downside and only a potential upside is worth exploring.

Summary

The general public has a large degree of skepticism about lawyers in general and the divorce process in particular. There is a popular myth that lawyers run up fees and overtry cases to the detriment of their clients. In an appropriate case, a signed cooperative divorce agreement may help alleviate some of this concern by assuring the parties that the attorneys intend to work toward a peaceful resolution of all issues involved.

Sample Form

Cooperative Divorce Agreement

The parties and their respective attorneys agree to handle this divorce on a cooperative basis. While they understand that this agreement is merely a statement of intent and not legally enforceable, they both commit in good faith to do the following:

1. Cooperate by acting civilly at all times and by responding promptly to all reasonable requests for information from the other party.
2. Cooperate by fully disclosing all relevant financial information as required by law.
3. Cooperate by obtaining joint appraisals and/or other expert opinions before obtaining individual appraisals or expert opinions.
4. Cooperate by obtaining meaningful expert input (e.g., child specialist) before requesting a custody study or the appointment of a guardian ad litem.
5. Cooperate in good faith negotiation sessions, including four-way sessions where appropriate, to reach fair compromises based on relevant information.
6. Cooperate by conducting themselves at all times in a respectful, civil, and professional manner.

Both parties and attorneys acknowledge that this agreement cannot be used against either party or attorney.

_____   _____
Husband   Date   Wife   Date

_____   _____
Attorney for Husband Date   Attorney for Wife   Date

Creative Settlement Techniques 17

Sometimes all the normal routes to settlement have failed. Yes, you could litigate the case, but a settlement is greatly preferable. Frequently, the client lacks the resources to pay for a trial. Some judges simply won't hear a divorce case (why did they want to become judges anyway?). Some judges would hear the trial but would make the experience so unpleasant that everyone is looking for another option. Some clients are terrified of court—maybe they watched too many lawyer TV shows or saw a few real trials. In any event, here are some ideas—some tested and some not—that might break the impasse when all else has failed.

Cut the Cookie

The oldest settlement trick in the book was devised by the greatest judge ever: the mother of multiple children. How do you divide a cookie so that each child gets half? Easy—one cuts, the other chooses.

Clearly, this is not a good idea when it comes to custody, but it can work in cases where there is property—

like personalty—that both parties want. Unless there is something that your client **must** have (the grandfather clock that has been in his family for seven generations), the "cookie cutter" technique can avoid a frequent ruling by trial courts on issues like personal property: sell everything.

Simply speaking, one party draws up two lists. The other chooses. Giving the other side the option keeps the list maker honest. This can work not only with personal property but also sometimes with cars, brokerage accounts, or other assets that either side could own. I even used this process once in a case where the parties owned six businesses, which they were each capable of running. My client divided the businesses into two lists of three businesses each and let the other side choose a list. It settled a difficult, contentious case in short order.

Of course, it is not always possible to equally divide businesses—or even personal property—into two lists, but sometimes just the exercise of preparing the lists can be conducive to settlement as it leads the parties to consider the comparative value of the property and to make choices.

The Buy-Sell Offer

In the right circumstances, making a "buy-sell" offer can resolve an issue. The right circumstances require an asset that can be awarded to either party with no adverse circumstances. Thus, this should not be an offer made by a husband who owns a business, knowing that his wife has no ability to run the business. That is not creative negotiating—that is manipulation.

On the other hand, ownership of certain assets is up for grabs. An example might be a car that one side is substantially undervaluing or overvaluing. In such a case, the other party might want to propose a value for which it would either accept the vehicle or agree that the vehicle be awarded to the other side.

This type of proposal is valuable where the only issue is the value of the asset, so it tends to work with cars, personal property items, and sometimes houses. After all, assuming that either party could own the assets with no ramifications, what could be more fair than to name a value and allow the other side to accept it at that value or not?

The Nontrial Trial

This technique requires four prerequisites:

- Two lawyers who trust each other and have reasonably good client control
- Two clients who understand the strategy and are willing to cooperate
- A cooperative court
- Disagreements that are over application of the facts, not over the facts themselves

The underlying basis of the "nontrial trial" is that many decisions by a trial court are discretionary. The "cooperative court" requirement entails a judge who is a known quantity and decides contested issues within discretionary limits. The theory behind this concept is that if both lawyers and their clients knew what the judge would do without a full-blown trial, they could simply tell their clients, who could then avoid the costs of a trial and just agree to the inevitable. After all, if the decision is within the trial court's discretion, then it is bulletproof on appeal anyway. (I know, I know—there are appellate decisions to the contrary. But let's deal with the norm rather than the exception.)

This technique is best utilized on the day of the trial since there is no going back, but it can also be used at pretrials. Whatever the purpose of the court date, the clients are informed in advance that the lawyers will present the issue informally to the judge. The judge must be a willing participant—some judges are and some are not—which requires assuring the judge that if the effort fails, neither side will ask the judge to recuse himself. The lawyers then informally argue the case before the judge and ask for his opinion. The judge will tell the lawyers what the ruling would likely be under those facts. The lawyers then tell their clients (if the conference is held in chambers), and the clients agree to the eventual order. In cases where the facts are not in dispute and the ruling is discretionary, the savings can be significant.

Some judges are uncomfortable with this approach as they are being asked to prejudge the case and therefore may have to disqualify themselves if the process fails. The potential for disqualification, however, is easily overcome. By virtue of the fact that they are asking the court for input, the parties are waiving the right to ask for disqualification if dissatisfied with the proposed order. Some courts will require this waiver on the record.

There is, of course, a well-recognized alternative dispute resolution technique of a mock trial that works very similarly to the nontrial trial except that it is far more formal and often includes calling witnesses and using the rules of evidence. Although this technique does have value in resolving cases, it is difficult to see how the costs are significantly less than a full trial before a court. In addition, since many issues in family court are highly discretionary, the findings of a mock court may be quite different than the findings of the judge who would ultimately hear the matter. Therefore, the technique suggested in this book is essentially a very informal variety of the mock trial, but one that would save time and costs by not utilizing the rules of evidence and by having the fact finder at the mock trial the same as the one at a real trial.

The danger in this technique rests in the waiver of any appellate remedies. Judges, of course, are subject to the same personal biases as everyone else, so if the particular judge needs to be constrained by the fear of a potential appeal, this is not a good technique for that case.

The Joint Recommendation

Earlier in this book, I described traditional, positional settlement negotiation, in which each side starts at polar opposites and then narrows the gap to finally settle someplace in between (see chapter 7, "Positional Negotiation"). Sometimes the narrowing of the gap is painfully slow as each side is afraid of bracketing the parameters. To get around an impasse, a joint recommendation by the attorneys may be a valuable settlement technique.

As with the nontrial trial, certain prerequisites are necessary for this technique to be successful:

- Lawyers with good client control
- Clients who won't undermine their attorneys
- A reasonable degree of trust between the attorneys

The concept works as follows: Each attorney privately ascertains from his client the range of acceptable settlements. The two lawyers meet, without clients, and discuss the remaining gap in positions. The lawyers agree on a final settlement number that is between the last two positions of the parties, although not necessarily halfway between. Each lawyer agrees to recommend the compromise to his client, understanding that if the client refuses to accept the joint recommendation, negotiations are over.

Clearly, the key to successfully making a joint recommendation is for each lawyer to know what settlement is acceptable to the client and not let the client change her mind later. Knowing that the joint recommendation is just that—a recommendation—neither lawyer prejudices himself if the client changes her mind. This is not a collaborative divorce.

The value of this technique is to reassure a client who is afraid of making too many compromises too fast, especially where the negotiations are getting very close to the final line but are not quite there yet. In these cases, sometimes knowing that the next compromise will be the last one gives the client enough assurance to authorize additional compromises.

Good faith rests in the finality of the joint recommendation. The lawyers are only going to recommend it to their clients, but the understanding is clear that failure to accept the joint recommendation means litigation—the lawyer has drawn the last line, and the joint proposal is the BATL (Best Alternative To Litigation).

Phone a Friend

Sometimes there is insufficient time or money for mediation or perhaps a judge who refuses to participate in the nontrial trial or other reasons why none of the above techniques will work. As with the television game show, it is a good idea to have a few friends on your contact list whom you can call upon in a pinch: conference calling a friend with the opposing counsel might help everyone involved get past a logjam, either by having the friend suggest a new approach or by expressing an independent opinion that causes one or both sides to compromise their position. Ideally, the friend will be one who is universally respected so that the other lawyer will respect his judgment. And, of course, the friend must be generous with his time. Such friends are rare, but they are out there, frequently willing to help without cost (although at least a thank-you note, if not a small gift, would be welcome).

The Curse of Too Much Money

Perhaps my favorite call from a client starts with "I have a real problem . . ."—but the "problem" turns out to be extra funds or found money. It can take the form of a significant tax refund, a bonus, a raise, an opportunity for overtime, or a second job. Of course, it is far more common that the problem is, in fact, a real problem, like a lost job or a cut in income. But in those good cases where the "bad" news is really one of timing, I will gasp and say, "How horrible! There is extra money to divide! What a curse!" (Sometimes clients will laugh—if they don't, *you* have a problem!)

The preferred way to deal with such a "curse" requires no creativity: pay bills (especially attorney fees)! But if that is not feasible or, as unusual as it may be, necessary, finding a creative use for such extra funds is not difficult. Perhaps it is due to funding three children through college at one time, but I've noticed that few parents have adequately funded their children's custodial or 529 plans, and this is a good place for at least a portion of the extra money. If not college accounts, then music lessons, sports activities, cars, insurance, and a myriad of other activities can be funded, even if only in the future through a formal or informal trust. Even if the spouses agree on little else, they can probably come to an understanding if the money will benefit the children directly.

The potential list of uses for such funds is endless. The real solution to this "problem" is to find a way to encourage whoever produced the money to continue to do so by deviating from the normal "divide-divide" methodology and finding creative ways of using the money that benefit everyone. All of our clients should have such problems!

Taking an Issue off the Table

Sometimes two issues become so inextricably linked that settlement becomes impossible. In such cases, a technique known as "taking an issue off the table" (see also chapter 13, "Family Law–Specific Settlement Issues") can work well.

As discussed in the chapter "Ethical Considerations," parties sometimes will improperly mix issues. The most common example is for women to resist additional visitation in order to coerce more child support from her spouse or for men to request more visitation in order to pay less child support to his spouse. Of course, lawyers should not promote marketing in children.

However, to accuse all men who request more time with the children as being motivated purely by financial considerations is as insulting—and wrong—as accusing all women who are resisting additional visitation of doing so for more support. And when the motivations are genuine, taking an issue off the table is a creative technique that can benefit settlement negotiations.

Although some clients are blatant about their motivations, it is not always easy to separate the honest negotiations from the manipulative ones. There is one method, albeit an imperfect one, of testing parties in cases where either you are unsure of a party's motivations or the other side is unfairly (in your opinion) questioning the motivations of your client. To illustrate how it works, let's use the male client seeking more visitation as an example. You would say to him: "Which is more important to you—more time with your children or paying less child support? In other words, if you cannot have both, which would you choose?" It is not always easy to get clients to make this choice; instead, many will argue that having to make this choice is not fair and will refuse to answer the question. If so, you have your answer, and the "taking an issue off the table" technique will not be an option.

However, if you have a client who chooses time over money, then try suggesting the following to the opposing lawyer:

Your client seems to suspect that her husband is not really interested in having the children more but only in paying less child support. To prove that she is wrong, he has authorized me to make the following proposal: We will deal with child support first, and he will pay the maximum amount of child support regardless of the visitation. Then, we will deal with the visitation, and your client can be comfortable that he sincerely wants time with the children and is not just seeking to pay less support.

Of course, this is not a perfect strategy. Many men will not clearly indicate their motivations. Regardless, some women will still see manipulation. However, there are cases in which unlinking issues can eliminate (or at least minimize) suspicion.

The "taking an issue off the table" technique is worth trying not just in child-support-versus-visitation cases but in any circumstances where there are linked issues and one is far more important to your client than the other. There are a myriad of examples involving personal property, such as collections or memorabilia, where the financial value is minimal but the emotional value is high. Sometimes taking such issues off the table at the beginning of negotiations can create an atmosphere for compromise. The cases where this may have particular value are those with a high degree of mistrust (that might be all of your cases!)—but not to the point of clinical paranoia, where no efforts at compromise will be understood or appreciated.

Acts of Loving Kindness

Here is an idea that will cause you to wonder if I'm living in the real world: See if you can convince your client at the outset of a case to do something nice for the other side. This works best if it would be totally unexpected by the other side. It would be easier to convince your client to do it if it is something that would cost your client little or nothing and is something that will happen eventually anyway.

One example: The husband moves out of the house, taking with him only his personal property. If you have a client who is not bitter and wants to resolve the case without rancor, suggest that, rather than waiting for the case to be over, she duplicate all family photos and videos and give them, unrequested, to her husband. It will cost her little to do so, she will have to do so eventually anyway, and it may create an atmosphere for settlement.

There are innumerable examples where such efforts may bear fruit. The concept is to dissipate (or at least diminish) the fear that your client is out for blood. Of course, if your client *is* out for blood, don't even think of it! But with the right client, in the right case, such a technique can have far-reaching benefits.

Summary

The above examples are by no means exclusive. I've heard of other creative settlement ideas, such as two lawyers breaking an impasse over $500 by each agreeing to compromise their fees by $250. One lawyer even told me that he made the final concession in a case once (presumably with his client's permission!) in exchange for a recipe for his favorite dinner. There are many, many other examples, and divorce lawyers should not be afraid to experiment and try to be creative. As long as the client is informed of the technique and it does not violate any ethical precept, go for it! Then, let others know if it worked so they can try it, too.

Divorce Settlements and Game Theory[1]

18

In her biography of John Nash, *A Beautiful Mind*, Sylvia Nasar described Nash's obsession with game theory, a mathematically based study of strategic decision making.[2] Although game theory involves extraordinarily complex mathematics, there is a basic correlation between game theory and divorce settlement negotiations that all family lawyers can understand. In fact, some game theory explains how divorce negotiations can be handled for the benefit of all involved.

Game Theory Background

Game theory studies the strategic interactions among rational players. (The problem in family law, of course, is immediately apparent. How many times are both "players"

---

1. This chapter was previously published in similar form in the following sources: Gregg Herman, *Math Games and Collaborative Law*, 4 COLLABORATIVE REV. 10 (Oct. 2002); and Gregg Herman, *Are Divorce Settlement Negotiations Like Games*, 18 AM. J. FAM. L. 5 (Spring 2004).
2. Sylvia Nasar, *A Beautiful Mind* (1998).

rational? Still, the lack of rationality is part of the study of game theory.) Game theory posits that these players will make choices that will lead to their best-expected payoffs given their knowledge and beliefs about the game at a given time. Put another way, game theory is all about the ways in which parties to any type of a decision can increase their payback when the others who are involved in the same game are also trying to do the same thing.

Research in the area of game theory began with an examination of games such as tic-tac-toe and chess, which Nash found "easy to analyse because they are games of 'complete information.'" Games of complete information are games that allow each player to see each other's position. After looking at these types of games for a while, mathematicians became interested in other games, such as poker. Poker "is much more interesting because [the] players cannot see each other's cards." It is not a game of complete information, and other elements of the game, like the bluff, can enter into the analysis.[3]

Eventually, Nash and other researchers studied "more important games." These other games included economics, warfare, and divorce settlement. It is interesting that these last three games are grouped together. In all of these games, there are two parties that are "competing over money [and/]or territory." Each party begins to develop a strategy that is "based on [a set of] strengths and objectives, and on the . . . mindset and skills of [its] opponent." Game theory became math plus psychology.[4]

The "Game" of Divorce

Game theory deals with psychology, i.e., how humans react to certain stimuli. In divorce settlement negotiations, lawyers are trying to get clients to react positively to a settlement proposal. Understanding game theory would be very helpful in settling cases. Thus, we are going to examine certain games and the applicability that they may have to divorce settlement negotiations.

---

3. Simon Singh, *The Great Game*, NEW STATESMAN (Mar. 25, 2002), *available at* http://www.newstatesman.com/node/142588 (last visited Oct. 15, 2012).
4. *Id.*

The Ultimatum Game

The following situation appeared for discussion on a family law attorney LISTSERV: The parties were divorced a few years ago. During the marriage, they filed joint income tax returns. The husband was awarded the business in the divorce. As a result of business losses after the divorce, the husband had losses that could result in a substantial refund if the parties filed amended joint income tax returns (it is not clear how the losses resulted in a refund for prior years, but please play along). The husband felt that since the adverse conditions occurred after the divorce at his expense, he should be entitled to the entire refund. The wife felt that since refunds were considered marital property and therefore divided equally, she should get half. If the parties could not agree, there would be no amended return and, therefore, no refund to divide at all.

This is a version of the game theory scenario known as "the ultimatum game." The ultimatum game is where two players interact to decide how to divide a sum of money that is given to them. In this game, one person (Player #1) is given a sum of money and proposes a division to the other player (Player #2). If Player #2 accepts the proposal, each player keeps his share. However, if Player #2 rejects the proposal, each player gets nothing.

From a rational perspective, Player #2 should accept any proposal made by Player #1 that is more than a penny. After all, one penny is better than nothing. Yet, actual experiments show that Player #2 almost always rejects proposals that are considered insultingly low. In other words, Player #2 would rather get nothing than take a proposed division that is not relatively close to equal, even though from a strictly rational economic point of view it makes no sense.

The lesson learned from the ultimatum game is that money is not the average person's sole motivation. If it were, Player #2 would always accept any offer of one penny or more.

For divorce lawyers, it is not at all uncommon to have a party—sometimes the lawyer's own client—turn down a proposal that is in the party's own interest. Occasionally, it is a lack of knowledge that causes people to act in a financially suicidal manner. Other times, other reasons come into play. How many times do divorce lawyers have clients who reject settlement proposals that might be to their economic advantage because those advantages are overshadowed by emotional considerations?

Texas Hold 'Em

Poker has become a staple of cable television. The most popular game is called "Texas Hold 'Em." The rules bear a remarkable similarity to divorce settlement negotiations. In Texas Hold 'Em, players are dealt two cards facedown ("hole" cards), while five cards are dealt faceup ("community" cards). The players bet, with the usual bluffing, of course. The winner is the player with the best five-card poker hand consisting of any combination of the player's hole cards with the community cards.

In divorce settlement, there are both community cards and hole cards. Both sides typically will know (or at least should know) some information, like the community cards in Texas Hold 'Em; in addition, both parties have information that they do not share with the other side—the equivalent of the hole cards. For example, both sides typically know the vocational history of both parties and their present income. However, their future plans may be secret. Therefore, in negotiations, they "play" with the known factors and hold back on the secrets. The resulting negotiations lead to suspicion and mistrust, which may affect the relationship of the parties far into the future.

Consider the following example: The husband is offered a new position with his company. Although accepting the position would result in substantially more income, it would also cause a major relocation and substantially increased hours and stress. As a result, a family court would not likely force him to accept the new position. The husband thinks that the job is only worth it if he does not have to share all of the financial benefits with his ex-wife. Although he is willing to accept sharing some of the additional benefits with her, there is a point where there would not be enough left over to balance out the negative attributes, such as relocation and the additional work requirements. The ex-wife, naturally, would like to share as much of the increased income as possible. However, if she asks to share too much, the husband will reject the new position, and she will get nothing. How much is too much? How much of the additional benefit would the husband need to keep to balance out the negatives of the new position? In standard negotiating strategy, both parties keep their positions close to the vest. Given sufficient suspicion and mistrust, the husband may simply reject the promotion, and both parties will lose.

This type of situation is common in family law, where cooperation can lead to better results for both parties. However, mistrust and lack of information often lead to worse results for both parties. For years, economists have studied these sorts of human interactions under the rubric of game theory.

The Prisoner's Dilemma

Another applicable game theory example is a famous puzzle known as "the prisoner's dilemma." Developed by one of Nash's professors at Princeton, the puzzle begins with the scenario that two people are arrested for the same crime.[5] Since the police do not have sufficient evidence to charge either one, they separate them for interrogation and try to get each one to turn state's evidence against the other. (Having served as an assistant district attorney for seven years, I can attest that this is exactly how real life works!) Each prisoner is told that the other one is betraying him and that it would be to the prisoner's advantage to cut a deal. The best scenario for the parties is if they cooperate with each other and refuse to talk to the police because they both will walk free. However, if one of them does not cooperate with the other but talks to the police, the defector will get a reduced sentence, and the other one will get full punishment. If they both talk, they will both be punished, but less severely than the prisoner who doesn't talk when his partner betrays him. The dilemma is that each prisoner has a choice between only two options—talk or don't talk—but cannot make a good decision without knowing what the other one will do.

This is precisely what happens in standard divorce negotiations. Both parties are meeting with their attorneys privately, each suspicious of what is going on with the other side. If they cooperate with each other, they have the best chance for optimal results for both. What typically happens instead is that the mistrust and lack of communication lead to the worst results for both. Being in separate attorney's offices while negotiating is akin to the prisoners being separated during interrogation.

Although the mathematics of the prisoner's dilemma is much more complex than what I've presented here, the basic concept is one that serves as the basis of the transparency of financial disclosure that is inherent in collaborative and cooperative divorce—and should

---

5. Merrill Flood and Melvin Dresher created the basis of the game. Albert W. Tucker crafted it into a scenario involving prisoners and christened it "the prisoner's dilemma."

happen in all cases. Understanding the basics of the prisoner's dilemma can assist lawyers in maximizing the benefits of a settlement to both parties—the win-win situation that is so difficult to actually attain.

Anchoring

Richard Thaler, who teaches at the University of Chicago, is considered the "godfather of behavioral economics."[6] Among the concepts that he has studied is "anchoring," which he described as follows:

> *And they had a wheel of fortune they spun with numbers between 0 and 100 and it would stop at some number, say 35, and they would say, "do you think the answer is above or below 35" and then "what do you think the answer is?" And people's answers were influenced by the number that came up on that wheel of fortune, even though they saw that the number was generated at random. So if you asked people, "do you think the percentage of African countries represented in the UN has anything to do with the number that came up on the wheel of fortune" they'd say "No, of course not. What are you, crazy?" But if they started at 35 they're gonna come up with a lower number than if they started at 85; its pretty much inevitable.*[7]

The application of anchoring, or using some point as a base on which to make or gauge future decisions, in divorce settlement relates to the issue of who makes the first offer. This is not to say that a lawyer should always (or never) make the first offer. Rather, when an offer is made, a lawyer should be aware of the psychological inclination to anchor that offer. By being aware of this tendency, a lawyer can make sure that any offer is weighed as much as possible in an objective sense by comparing it to the BATNA rather than to an anchor point planted in the client's psyche.

---

6. *The Days of Wine and Mouses: Transcript*, FREAKONOMICS RADIO (Mar. 17, 2012) (quoting Stephen J. Dubner), http://www.wnyc.org/shows/freakonomics-radio/2012/mar/17/transcript/ (last visited Oct. 14, 2012).
7. *Id.* (quoting Richard Thaler).

Zero Sum or Nonzero Sum

Another mathematics game described in Nasar's book is the "zero sum game." In such a game, in order for one player to win, another player has to lose. A poker game is an example of a zero sum game. In a "nonzero sum game," on the other hand, all of the players may benefit. Some of Nash's Nobel Prize–winning work involved using non-zero sum games to describe the working of a nation's economy, where everyone can benefit from growth.[8]

The application to divorce is obvious. Most cases are zero sum games. The more the payer pays, the less he has. Wouldn't it be nice to negotiate a settlement that expands the available pie rather than divides it? In the above example of the husband who has an opportunity for a more lucrative job, if the husband takes the higher-paying job, more money is available for both parties. More typically, by shifting tax responsibility, parties can sometimes turn divorce into a nonzero sum game by creating more money to divide between the parties.

Why are divorce negotiations usually played as a zero sum game? Again, the mistrust between the parties frequently causes one party to believe that "any money going to the other party must come from me."

Utilization of Game Theory in Divorce

How can game theory be utilized in divorce? As discussed in this book, in order for divorces to be handled on a cooperative or a collaborative basis, both parties must voluntarily disclose all of their interests without the need for formal discovery. In other words, all of the cards are immediately put on the table—there are no hole cards. The parties jointly hire all appraisers. Settlement negotiations are transparent, usually through four-way meetings with the parties and their attorneys.

Whether via a cooperative approach or a full-blown collaborative approach, by placing the hole cards of Texas Hold 'Em face up, the prisoner's dilemma is eliminated because the negotiations take place in the open rather than in secret. Thus, the divorce "game" becomes a larger game than zero sum, to the benefit of all involved.

Other game theory methodologies hopefully will develop over the years. Such as-yet-undiscovered methods can look to other disciplines—in the same way that game theory is currently based in economics,

---

8. NASAR, *supra* note 2.

psychology, and mathematics—in order to help parties avoid the lose-lose scenarios so common in divorce. Perhaps game theory will someday look at the playground scenario where children are told, "You are all winners." In divorce, both parties can be winners as well.

Summary

Game theory provides research and data on the psychology of negotiations. Various aspects of game theory are applicable to divorce negotiations, so the study of game theory can aid lawyers in understanding the psychology involved in settlement and thus lead to favorable results for everyone.

Ethical Considerations 19

In the practice of law, attorneys face numerous ethical dilemmas when dealing with clients and opposing parties. For family law attorneys, there are special concerns. Family law attorneys are usually dealing with extremely emotional clients with significant problems within the most personal aspects of their lives: their family and home. As discussed in this book, emotions often alter clients' rational decision-making abilities. During these cases, it can become easy for an attorney to face various family law–related ethical dilemmas.

Some of the most common ethical situations that family law attorneys will face include their ability to lie about material facts regarding their clients' intentions to settle and their right to withdraw from a case. What sometimes seems immoral or unfair to a client or opposing party can still be ethical according to the ABA's *Model Rules of Professional Conduct*.

This chapter will cover several ethical considerations that crop up frequently in family law. For a comprehensive set of rules (with comments) related to family law issues, the best source is *Bounds of Advocacy*, published by the American Academy of Matrimonial Lawyers.[1]

Truthfulness

Settlement negotiations have some unique ethical considerations. The most striking consideration is, as strange as it might sound, that an attorney is allowed to lie under certain circumstances. However, it is important to understand the limitations of those circumstances.

ABA Model Rules

The ABA has noted that a lawyer shall not "make a false statement of a material fact or law to a third person."[2] Specifically, "[a] lawyer is required to be truthful when dealing with others on a client's behalf. . . . A misrepresentation can occur if the lawyer incorporates or affirms a statement of another person that the lawyer knows is false."[3] However, the ABA clarified that there are rare circumstances when an attorney can lie: "Under generally accepted conventions in negotiation, certain types of statements ordinarily are not taken as statements of material fact. *Estimates of price or value placed on the subject* of a transaction and *a party's intention* as to an acceptable settlement of a claim are ordinarily in this category."[4]

Material Facts versus Clients' Intentions

Using an example of a personal injury action because the issues are clearer than in a divorce action, we can see when lying is acceptable. Let's say a personal injury (PI) attorney assesses the value of a claim at $100,000. When the lawyer discusses it with the client, the client agrees to accept a settlement at that value. In fact, the client may even tell the lawyer that is all that she wants. However, the PI attorney may call the insurance lawyer and demand a settlement of $200,000, asserting that the client will not accept one cent less. The lawyer is lying: the client

---

1. BOUNDS OF ADVOCACY (Am. Acad. of Matrimonial Lawyers 1991), *available at* http://www.aaml.org/library/publications/19/bounds-advocacy (last visited Oct. 14, 2012).
2. MODEL RULES OF PROF'L CONDUCT R. 4.1(a) (2001).
3. *Id.* R. 4.1 cmt. 1.
4. *Id.* R. 4.1 cmt. 2 (emphasis added).

has already professed a willingness to settle for half that amount. Yet, in settlement negotiations, the attorney is acting in a perfectly ethical manner.

On the other hand, if the PI attorney told the insurance adjuster that the claim was worth $200,000 because the client had a broken leg when, in fact, the client really only had a sprained ankle, the lawyer would be acting unethically. The difference is that in the first situation, the lawyer is misrepresenting the intentions of the client regarding settlement of claims; and in the second situation, the lawyer is misrepresenting a material fact. The former is appropriate; the latter is not.

Although the client must agree to the attorney's strategies, this is not a difficult sell. The general concept of asking for more to get less—or the converse—is intuitive. However, as part of the settlement conference with the client, the lawyer should explain this strategy. In addition, although attorneys, of course, appreciate the difference between lying about material facts and lying about a party's settlement intentions, clients may not be aware of the distinction and may believe that attorneys can and will lie about anything to win the case. Therefore, it is essential for the attorney to explain to the client where the line is drawn, i.e., the ethical differences between material facts and nonmaterial facts.

Withdrawal

Early in my career as a divorce lawyer, a client decided to accept a settlement offer that I felt was very much against her interests. I could not talk her out of it. She testified at the hearing that she understood that her attorney did not recommend the agreement and that she was accepting it against my advice. Still, several years later, I learned that she testified in a postjudgment motion that she accepted the agreement only because her lawyer recommended it. Ever since, on the rare occasion when a client wants to accept a proposal that I believe would be against her interests, I have threatened to withdraw or actually have withdrawn from representation.

What should an attorney do when he feels that the client is no longer acting in a rational manner and proceeding in the case would go against the logical and moral stance of the firm and/or attorney? According to the *Model Rules of Professional Conduct*, "a lawyer *may* withdraw from representing a client if . . . the client insists upon taking action that the lawyer considers repugnant or with which the lawyer has a fundamental disagreement; . . . or other good cause for withdrawal exists."[5]

When an attorney is considering withdrawing from a case, there are certain things that the attorney must do. First, the attorney must know whether the particular court allows withdrawal after notice or if permission from the tribunal to terminate the representation is required. Second, the attorney must remember that withdrawal cannot cause a material adverse effect on the client's interest.[6]

When to Leave

The difficult issue is to differentiate between when the attorney must withdraw and when the attorney should withdraw. The former is a matter of ethics; the latter is a matter of propriety.

A determination of when to leave is somewhat subjective. Certainly, if the client is committing fraud, there is little subjectivity involved. However, a more difficult, and I would suggest more common, circumstance occurs when the client's directions in terms of settlement would be self-destructive but not fraudulent.

An example would be a case involving a woman with whom I met for possible representation in a paternity case. She hit the "sperm jackpot," being pregnant with a child of an extremely highly paid professional athlete. When I say *extremely highly paid*, I am not exaggerating *the extremely* part. She came to the meeting with her idea of an appropriate settlement. It was not even close to what she could expect. In sports terms, if there is a fifty-yard line for settlement, you couldn't even see the stadium from her "kickoff point." From an ethical point of view, as long as the lawyer does not represent to the client that the proposal is reasonable, there is no prohibition in making an extremely high initial (or even later) proposal. Whether this is a smart idea is, of course, a very different question.

This is a chapter on ethics, not strategy, so it is important to point out that the circumstances in which the client insists on a settlement that is not fraudulent but not good strategy do not require withdrawal. Still, the lawyer may choose to do so. Why? Several reasons. For one,

---

5. *Id.* R. 1.16(b)(4), (7) (emphasis added).
6. *Id.* R. 1.16(b)(7)(c), (d).

the lawyer may decide that making a silly proposal detracts from the lawyer's own credibility. My law firm, for example, has been practicing family law for fifty years. Hopefully, in that time, we have earned the right to be taken seriously. Good reputations take years to earn and can be lost quickly. We have no intention of allowing one client to detract from this reputation. So, rather than making a proposal that is not going to be taken seriously, we might tell the client that we would be taking her money needlessly and will withdraw unless the client reconsiders.

How to Leave

Knowing how to leave—and how to leave without creating ethical and financial problems for yourself and your client—is even more important than knowing when to leave.

In terms of how to leave, there are two types of withdrawals: the "noisy" withdrawal and the "normal" withdrawal.

A noisy withdrawal is most common when the client wants to commit or have the lawyer commit an ethical breach. In this case, the lawyer cannot ethically continue to represent the client. At the same time, the withdrawal cannot disclose attorney-client privileged information. Until the attorney has formally withdrawn from the case, he must remember that he is still that client's attorney and must continue to represent the client effectively and competently. This is not always easy as the lawyer may have to walk a tightrope between withdrawing and withdrawing without violating any confidence.

The normal withdrawal is easy and should be seamless. This type of withdrawal assumes that there is no trial date coming soon or other reason that a court might refuse to allow a withdrawal, and the reasons for withdrawal are due to strategy rather than ethics. In any circumstance, the lawyer needs to remember several things. First, the file belongs to the client. If the client requests her file, the attorney must surrender the documents to the client or the newly appointed attorney. However, the attorney can make copies of the file if he believes it necessary for proof of representation or fees. Next, the attorney must remain professional at all times. Furthermore, the attorney must make sure that all correspondence is in writing and limited to what needs to be said so that that client can move on with her case. Finally, the attorney must inform the client of any approaching deadlines. By taking these actions, attorneys will protect their reputation and most likely avoid having any ethical grievances filed against them.

Collaborative Law

Collaborative divorce, an alternative to dispute resolution, allows parties to divorce with dignity, respect, and cooperation. In short, collaborative law is when the parties agree to openly discuss all relevant information and to negotiate everything honestly and openly with their attorneys. Furthermore, they agree that they will *not* litigate the case but will bring in accountants, therapists, mediators, and financial planners to help settle disputes that cannot be made among the parties and their attorneys.

In 2007, shock waves went around the collaborative law community when the Ethics Committee of the Colorado Bar Association issued an opinion finding that collaborative law violates ethical rule 1.7(b).[7] The Colorado bar believed that the four-way agreement, which the parties contractually agree to sign, cannot be validly obtained.

This opinion has been criticized by numerous practitioners and has not been followed by any other state ethics board.[8] The ABA issued a formal opinion disagreeing with the Colorado bar and specifically finding that the process is acceptable under the *Model Rules of Professional Conduct*.[9]

It is no wonder the Colorado opinion remains isolated. The key to protecting the client in a collaborative divorce is to give full disclosure of the risks. This is no different from other legal decisions that are made in the course of representation where the client is entitled to full disclosure of the risks before making a decision.

One of the strongest arguments for collaborative divorce is that a settlement-based approach in many cases is conducive not only to protection of a child but also to a preferable economic settlement for

---

7. Colo. Bar Ass'n Ethics Comm., Op. No. 115 (Feb. 24, 2007) (finding that collaborative law violates COLO. RULES OF PROF'L CONDUCT Old R. 1.7(b) (amended Jan. 1, 1997)).
8. This criticism is in addition to my primary complaint, which is that when citing to an article that I cowrote about collaborative divorce, the bar committee misspelled my name. That should nullify the opinion in and of itself!
9. Am. Bar Ass'n, Op. No. 07-447 (Aug. 9, 2007).

both parties. In mediation, fear of litigation may, in certain cases, lead to financial concessions. A settlement-based process can lead to fuller disclosure (what collaborative lawyers call "transparency"), more creative settlement approaches, and recognition of the economic interconnections of the parties. In fact, it can appeal to the parties' best instincts rather than their worst fears.

If the client's primary interest is to protect the child and there is a methodology of practice that is designed to best accomplish this goal, is it ethical **not** to offer this option to a potential client in an appropriate case?

Respect for the Opposing Side

According to family law attorney John Mayoue, professionalism in settlement negotiations involve civility, integrity, and respect. These attributes, rather than being contrary to the client's interests, are consistent with them because they avoid polarizing the parties and their positions. It is a lack of professionalism toward the other side and the other party that makes it difficult to settle cases and is, therefore, contrary to the client's interests.[10]

ABA rules specify that lawyers owe a duty of respect, courtesy, and fair dealing to the other side of a case. This means that in the conduct of negotiations, a lawyer should "conduct himself or herself with dignity and fairness and refrain from conduct meant to harass the opposing party. A lawyer should not advance groundless claims, defenses and objections."[11]

Lawyers should avoid the all-too-common situation of being pulled into an emotional maelstrom in the highly emotionally charged area of family law. For one thing, it is not effective advocacy. Taking on the opposing counsel as an enemy is not a strategy that is conducive to a positive settlement. In addition, respect for opposing counsel is consistent not only with principles of professionalism but also with ethical requirements.

---

10. John Mayoue, *Professional Comportment in Settlement, in* THE JOY OF SETTLEMENT 143, 143–45 (Gregg Herman ed., 1997).
11. N.J. STATE BAR ASS'N, PRINCIPLES OF PROFESSIONALISM (2010).

Respect should be manifested in the following ways:

- At a minimum, never—and I mean NEVER—raise your voice unless the opposing lawyer has a hearing issue—not a "listening" problem but a real hearing problem. Raised voices don't promote getting to "yes."
- Never make the discussion personal. The following comments (and worse!) are unlikely to promote compromise: "No wonder you have such a bad reputation." "Are you really taking your client's money for this?" "Did you actually go to law school?"
- In a four-way meeting, never address the other lawyer's client directly unless the other lawyer consents.

A number of years ago, I learned a valuable lesson from a colleague. We got into a discussion over the telephone regarding a difficult issue. As the conversation became heated, my colleague said, "Gregg, stop talking. We are both going to hang up now and talk again in twenty-four hours. Are you available then?" I was, and twenty-four hours later we resumed the discussion and resolved the issue. When I asked him why he had insisted on the cooling-off period, he said, "Gregg, we were both getting angry; and when we are angry, we stop listening to each other. If neither of us is listening, there is no way we are going to reach an agreement."

Communication with Clients

Some proposals in the field are too ridiculous to be taken seriously. As W. C. Fields said, "I'll see what my lawyer says. . . . And if he says yes, I'll get another lawyer."[12]

ABA Model Rule 1.4 requires lawyers to keep a client "reasonably informed about the status of the matter" and to explain matters sufficiently to allow the client to make informed decisions.[13] Thus, even those ridiculous proposals need to be passed along to our clients. Of course, as lawyers, we make recommendations to clients, and we may very well recommend rejecting a proposal. Still, the final decision

---

12. WinWisdom Quotations, W. C. Fields Quotes, http://www.winwisdom.com/quotes/author/w-c-fields-4.aspx (last visited Oct. 31, 2012).
13. Model Rules of Prof'l Conduct R. 1.4(a)(3), 1.4(b) (2001).

belongs to the client. Therefore, the client always needs to be informed of any settlement proposal, no matter how outlandish it may seem.

This does not make the lawyer a prisoner of the client's decision. If, as sometimes happens, a client decides to accept a proposal that is very much against her interests, the lawyer can—and should—withdraw from representation, subject to ethical rules discussed earlier in this chapter.

Improper Mixing

There are issues that should not be mixed. We are, of course, living in the real world where clients will sometimes try to seek concessions by improper mixing. Lawyers need to discourage this behavior and negotiate accordingly.

The most common example of improper mixing in family law involves a child support–visitation trade-off (see chapter 13, "Family Law–Specific Settlement Issues" and "Creative Settlement Techniques"). This improper trade-off has many varieties. In the most typical situation, a mother will resist visitation if the father does not agree to pay what she views as sufficient child support. Alternatively, a father will request additional visitation not so much because he wants to be with his children but because he wishes to pay less child support. There are endless variations, sometimes quite blatant. Any way these issues are mixed is ethically wrong as it constitutes marketing in children.

Obviously, not all parents either resisting additional visitation or asking for more visitation are doing so for unethical reasons. Still, as divorce lawyers, we should not pretend that such improper mixing does not occur. And, of course, we should never encourage it; rather, we should discourage it, consistent with Rule 5.2 of *Bounds of Advocacy*.[14]

Summary

Although rules of professional conduct apply to family attorneys in the same manner as they apply to all attorneys, there are certain

---

14. "An attorney should advise the client of the potential effect of the client's conduct on a child custody dispute." BOUNDS OF ADVOCACY R. 5.2 (Am. Acad. of Matrimonial Lawyers 1991), *available at* http://www.aaml.org/library/publications/19/bounds-advocacy (last visited Oct. 14, 2012).

considerations in family law that warrant special attention. When family law attorneys represent parents, they need to keep in mind the effect of the case on the children, whether minors or adults, and conduct themselves accordingly.

Ten Commandments[1] 20

There is a wonderful scene in the movie *Butch Cassidy and the Sundance Kid*. Robert Redford is going to fight the head of a gang for supremacy, but first he suggests that they discuss the rules for the fight. When the much bigger and meaner opponent drops his knife to his side to ask, incredulously, "What? Rules? In a knife fight?" Redford uses the opportunity to kick him in a very sensitive part of the male anatomy.[2]

Usually, parties are going through a divorce because there is a lack of trust, communication, and cooperation in the marriage. When a legal action starts and lawyers get involved, this lack of trust, communication, and cooperation does not lessen. Rather, it usually gets worse. However, a certain degree of trust, communication, and cooperation are necessary to reach a settlement.

---

1. This chapter was previously published, in whole or in part, in several sources, including Gregg Herman, *Divorce Settlement Negotiations*, 17:7 GEN. PRAC., SOLO & SMALL FIRM DIV. MAG., Oct./Nov. 2000, at 34.
2. BUTCH CASSIDY AND THE SUNDANCE KID (Twentieth Century Fox 1969).

Paradoxically, the very reasons that bring the parties to the bargaining table are the major impediments to settlement.

As a result, some basic rules are needed in the divorce "knife fight." The parties need to overcome the fundamental impediments to settlement instead of kicking each other. The following are a few suggested rules—"Ten Commandments"—for lawyers to adopt to help make sure that everyone's private parts are protected.

Rule One: Be Cordial

There is an old saying that you can catch more flies with honey than with vinegar. This is a lesson that lawyers need to teach their clients. The parties are used to dealing with each other by yelling and screaming. However, the lawyer should not posture in front of the client and should tell the client that he will not posture.

This is not as simple as it sounds. Unfortunately, television has conditioned many clients to believe that cordial conduct is not what to expect from a lawyer. The TV lawyer postures, threatens, intimidates, and is rude. Then the other side backs down—and cut to a commercial. Clients need to be told that effective advocacy does not mean putting on a show for the client's benefit.

It would be nice, but naïve, to think that it is sufficient merely to be cordial. However, family law practitioners do not practice law in a vacuum. In family law, the attorneys need to carefully consider every step they take due to the fact that the parties have such an incredibly large emotional stake in the litigation. It is this emotional stake, along with the misconception regarding attorneys, that causes the parties to want to emotionally involve the lawyer.

To deal with this, the lawyer needs to carefully explain to the client at the outset the reason for a cordial atmosphere with opposing counsel. In some cases, the client will take this well—and, in fact, the client may want nothing else. Often, though, the client will be quite shocked that the lawyer wants to be polite to the "enemy."

The lawyer can use any of several different explanations to convince the client that cordiality is the best strategy. The explanation for cordiality may be based on increasing the likelihood of settlement. After all, most clients want their cases settled. These clients will appreciate being reminded that settlement is easier if both sides behave cordially rather than with threats and intimidation. Other clients can be reached through their pocketbooks. If lawyers maintain civility toward each other, it is far easier to pick up the phone and discuss issues. If they cannot do so, then the result is innumerable court hearings. It is obviously far cheaper to have a phone conversation than to go to court. The explanation that works will, obviously, depend on the individual client. What is important is that the lawyer explain the strategy to the client at the outset.

Rule Two: Do Not Give Ultimatums

Certainly, some issues are more important than others. There may even be issues that are nonnegotiable. But stating these in the form of an ultimatum will stop the negotiating process in its tracks.

Which of the following tactics, for example, is more likely to bring about a measured response leading to discussions of settlement and compromise?

Approach A: Here is a settlement proposal. You have forty-eight hours to accept it, or it is withdrawn.

Approach B: Here is a settlement proposal. It contains what we believe to be reasonable positions on all issues. If you or your client disagrees, then please provide us with the reasons you disagree and what you think would be reasonable under the circumstances.

Clearly, Approach A puts the other side on the defensive. It is essentially asking for a fight, and most lawyers do not need more than one invitation. On the other hand, Approach B is far more likely to bring out the type of reasonable discourse that can lead to a settlement.

Rule Three: Do Not Give Deadlines

On occasion, I have received settlement proposals with "sunsets" of, for example, 5:00 p.m. on a particular Friday. A sunset is really a threat—an ultimatum—which brings out the type of response discussed in Rule Two. Usually, these are not great proposals anyway; after all, if the proposal was really that great, there would be no need for the sunset.

When the other side gives a "Friday at 5:00 p.m." deadline, try the following response:

Dear Joe:

My client was going to accept your proposal on Friday when she noticed that it was 5:10 p.m. See you in court.

As noted, if the offer was that great for your client, the other side would not have had to resort to threats. And if the offer was not that great, then nothing is lost by not responding. When I have used this tactic, the other lawyer usually calls me and offers to extend the deadline. I then take the opportunity to explain to the other lawyer that the issue is not the particular time, it is that I do not want to be given a deadline.

Instead of sending threatening deadlines to the other side, try this instead:

Dear Joe:

I promise that I won't threaten you during the settlement process, and I request that you don't threaten me.

In any event, if you want the case settled, do not use deadlines any more than you would use any other type of threat or ultimatum.

Rule Four: Make Full Disclosure Voluntarily and Freely

Ask yourself this question: Are you more likely to settle a case when the other side has given you everything that you need voluntarily, freely, and openly or when they stonewall discovery? The answer is obvious. When the other side treats financial information as if it were a highly classified government secret, settlement is less likely. This tactic brings out the "What are they trying to hide?" question. This sort of mistrust is not conducive to settlement.

Furthermore, there is always the ugly aspect of risking malpractice in recommending a settlement to a client based upon insufficient discovery information. If a lawyer does not believe that he has full disclosure, it is the lawyer's insurance on the line if the lawyer recommends a settlement. Many a lawyer will recommend a trial rather than a settlement to avoid such a risk.

Here is a tactic that my office has used with great success in encouraging settlement: When you represent the side with all of the information, give it to the other side *before* it asks. After all, you know what the other side will need in order to settle the case. Instead of waiting for the initial request for tax returns, retirement plan information, and the like, have your client compile it. Then give it to the other side, organized and indexed. Tell the other side that you are doing it to promote an atmosphere for settlement and to save costs for both parties. You should also explain that the information is not exclusive and that your client will be pleased to provide any additional relevant information that you might have inadvertently omitted.

By providing this information even before a request is made, you will have accomplished at least two positive things. First, if the other side requests a court intervention regarding discovery, the court will be impressed by the voluntary provision of large amounts of financial documentation. At least in my jurisdiction, family courts dislike discovery motions and routinely order everything to be provided unless absolutely outrageous. Second, and more important, voluntarily providing the information creates the type of atmosphere that allows opposing counsel to enter into settlement negotiations without the paranoia inherent in the cases in which the stonewall approach is used.

Rule Five: Don't Be Afraid of Taking the First Step

Some lawyers fear that making the first step toward settlement is a sign of weakness. As a result, some cases sit and wait, whereas a settlement conference can begin the process of resolution. As discussed by Mark Sullivan in *The Joy of Settlement*, timing is everything in settlement.[3] To miss the timing because of a fear of appearing weak does the client no good.

To put it another way, someone has to take the first step, or no case will ever be settled. To view this first step as a sign of weakness is a sign of insecurity on the part of the lawyer. On the other hand, taking the first step can be a sign of strength: the lawyer appears so confident in his case that the other side will want to settle to avoid the embarrassment of the presumed eventual defeat in court.

---

3. Mark Sullivan, *Time Problems, in* AM. BAR ASS'N, THE JOY OF SETTLEMENT 138 (Gregg M. Herman ed., 1997).

There have been several times in my career that I have almost missed an opportunity due to stubbornness, arrogance, or, maybe, insecurity. Once, for example, we were in court on the day of trial because all previous efforts at settlement had failed. Communication had ceased several weeks before even though we had made an offer that we were amazed was not accepted. Typical of most court hearings, a lengthy delay preceded the hearing while the court dealt with other matters. During the delay, I mentioned to my client that our last proposal was really a win-win offer and should have been accepted. My client said that perhaps I should bring it up again to the other lawyer while we were waiting. Every aspect of my ego said no, that the offer was rejected and to ask again was a sign of weakness. Nonetheless, at my client's prodding, I approached the other lawyer and told her that our prior offer was still open. She thanked me and spoke to her client—and they accepted the offer. We never did find out why they did not accept the offer initially or approach us first during the wait in court. What is clear is that if I had not listened to my client and overcome my ego, a win-win settlement would not have occurred.

Rule Six: Never Negotiate Backward

Backward negotiating is what occurs when, say, the initial offer by a plaintiff is for $100,000 and the second offer is for $200,000. Backward negotiating also happens when a defendant's offer, once rejected as too low, goes lower in subsequent offers.

There are times when facts change, which may alter settlement positions. However, assuming that discovery was conducted before settlement (as it should be), once a proposal is made, subsequent proposals should be closer to the other side's position—not farther away.

Backward negotiating is a form of intimidation. It tells the people on the other side that they are idiots for not jumping at the initial offer and that subsequent offers will be less unless they jump at the present offer. Although those on the other side may in fact be idiots, it is not conducive to settlement to educate them to that fact. After all, lawyers, like everyone else, do not like being told that they are idiots (perhaps especially if it is true). A lawyer's reaction to such an opinion is far more likely to be rolling up sleeves for a fight than proving the opinion by caving in to backward negotiating.

Moreover, backward negotiating is not good faith negotiating, and the response of a party that receives a backward offer should be to stop negotiating. If a proposal is made in good faith, then the rug should not be pulled out from under it.

In effective negotiations, the object is for both lawyers to look good to their respective clients. By negotiating backward, the message to the other spouse is that her lawyer made a mistake in not recommending a previous settlement offer. Although that might be true, the opposing counsel is unlikely to admit the mistake. Rather, the usual reaction of opposing counsel in such circumstances is to want to go to trial to prove that he was right in turning down the proposal. Some lawyers do not agree that they have any responsibility to make the other lawyer look good. Those are the lawyers who end up in trial the most often. For those lawyers who prefer to settle cases, the ego of the opposing counsel is a factor that needs to be considered.

I know of a lawyer who is an outstanding negotiator. Every offer he makes is made from the perspective of not just what is right for his client but also how the lawyer on the other side will treat the offer. His theory is that if the other lawyer has room to get more for his client, that lawyer will be a hero to the client and aggressively pursue settlement. Almost all of his cases settle.

Rule Seven: Never Refuse to Negotiate

True, some cases are harder to settle than others, and some cannot be settled. But you will never know unless you try. Yes, it may turn out later that some legal services thought necessary at the time were avoidable. Nonetheless, settlement should be attempted in every case no matter how remote the prospect might seem.

Why do some lawyers refuse to negotiate? Sometimes it is because of personality conflicts with the other lawyer. No question, some lawyers grate on each other. However, no law has ever required settlement negotiations to be conducted in person. Using written negotiations takes most (although not all) of the personality conflicts out of the equation. I have seen cases where the parties actually get along better than their lawyers! In fact, I know of cases where the parties could have settled if left to their own devices. Although this is exceedingly rare in my experience, it should never happen. Lawyers should be conduits for settlement, not impediments.

Another reason that lawyers sometimes refuse to negotiate is that they perceive the gap between the positions as too wide to "waste" time negotiating. Even sitting down for negotiations seems to be a waste of time. Yet, it is amazing the number of times the gap narrows dramatically during a negotiations session. Sometimes the gap was there at the beginning only for positioning. Sometimes a party recognizes the weakness of its position after negotiations begin. The point is that the gap cannot narrow unless there is some negotiating.

This does not mean, of course, that it is never proper to walk out of a negotiating session, suspend negotiations, or even stop negotiations. It does mean that is improper to never enter into negotiations at all. At least sit down with the other lawyer and see what is on his mind. And do not stand on ceremony—again, making the first call is not a sign of weakness. In fact, the reluctance to call reminds me of the teenage boy afraid to call the girl for fear of rejection, while the girl sits by the phone hoping for the call but too timid to call on her own.

Rule Eight: Never Get Personal

There is a scene in *The Godfather* where a character is about to wiped out by the mob. One of the henchmen tells the victim that the Godfather wants him to know that it is not personal—it is just business.[4]

Clearly, much of what is happening in a divorce is personal between the parties. However, it should never be personal between the attorneys, no matter how sensitive or important the issues. Most times, this is not a problem. The vast majority of the lawyers with whom I deal are pleasant, and I consider many of them to be friends. It is only a very small minority of lawyers with whom I must make a real effort to maintain civility.

There is no benefit in being hostile. In nearly twenty years of practice, I have never had a confrontational conversation with an attorney who said the following: "Gregg, I am wrong, you are right. Can you forgive me for taking such a silly position?"

A good rule of thumb for negotiations: Never fight a battle; the best you can do is tie. In court, with a judge present, there is at least a chance of winning. In a private discussion with the other lawyer, there is absolutely no chance. At best, there will be a standoff.

---

4. THE GODFATHER (Paramount Pictures 1972).

There are times when I temporarily terminate a conversation in order to control my temper (my wife will be surprised to learn that I even have a temper). Even an abrupt termination of a conversation is preferable to saying what may be on my mind.

Rule Nine: Never Get Angry at a Settlement Proposal

If a settlement proposal comes in writing, my firm immediately sends it out to the client. It is not unusual that the client calls us after reading, livid with anger at the outrageousness of the proposal and how far the proposal is from what the client perceives as fair.

True, some proposals are so low or so high as to be insulting. Some lawyers ask for the stars hoping to get the moon. Others misinterpret the parameters of reasonable settlement. Whichever is true, though, at least there is an attempt at settlement. Rather than get angry, if the proposal is in the stars, then start subterranean (or whatever is the opposite of the stars!). If the proposal is unreasonable due to a misunderstanding of reality, then educate the other side. But never get angry—any proposal, even a bad one, is better than no proposal at all.

Rule Ten: Be Prepared!

Going into settlement negotiations without a prior face-to face meeting with your client is as wrong as going into trial without such a meeting. Worse, it wastes the time and money of not only your client but also the lawyer and the client on the other side. Spend time with the client to discuss starting points and ending points for negotiations. Make sure the client understands that although settlement negotiations are, in many ways, the equivalent of a knife fight, there are rules that will be followed.

If you make a habit out of not being prepared for settlement negotiations, you will earn a reputation for not being prepared. My reaction to lawyers with this reputation is to not prepare myself for the negotiation session. The result is that it is far less likely that the case will be settled. On the other hand, if I know that the lawyer on the other side prepares hard for settlement, I will work hard as well. The result is a good session that will make great progress toward a resolution, if not reach one.

True, there are some lawyers who bluff well, but most do not. The degree of preparation of the other side is usually clear early in the negotiating session. In many settlement conferences, after both sides lay out their positions, there is a palpable pause as both sides hesitate to see who will make the first compromise. If it is clear that one side is not prepared, why would the other side start to compromise? By not being prepared to negotiate, the one side is not prepared to match the other side's compromises. The result is a standoff. The bottom line is to follow the Boy Scout motto: Be prepared!

Summary

Following these rules does not, of course, guarantee a settlement. They do, however, create the type of atmosphere that makes a settlement more likely. As with many other things in life, improving the odds is often the best that we can when we do not have full control over the circumstances—and we owe it to our clients to do the best that we can.

The Endgame 21

Unfortunately, no matter how good the negotiators, not all cases are resolved. There is a reason that courthouses were built, and it was not for rubber-stamping settlement agreements. What is the point at which you should simply walk away? And how do you devise your BATNA (see chapter 1, "*Getting to YES*: Traditional Theory") so that you know when you get there?

The Client Knows Best

It must be recognized that it is the client's decision, not the lawyer's decision, to accept a deal or walk away. As any experienced attorney can attest, there are occasions when the client is smarter than the lawyer, and rejecting a recommended settlement works to that client's advantage. And vice versa.

One client of mine was a successful business owner who, although maybe not quite ruthless, bargained tough. By the time of trial, for a series of complex reasons, we were in a far stronger position for settlement—or, for that matter, litigation. At the last minute, the other side, clearly recognizing its dilemma, made a settlement proposal just slightly above our bottom line. I wanted to reject it. My client stopped me. "Take it," he ordered. When I asked him why, he responded, "That's the mother of my children." This was the first time he had expressed any softness toward her in the entire process. When we did our postmortem on the negotiations, he told me that although he knew he could do better—maybe even significantly better—at trial, there was a certain value for his wife in thinking that he had caved. We will never know if the future would have been different otherwise. However, in his case, as his business prospects improved, she never asked for additional support; and any minor issues relating to custody, placement, or finances were resolved easily. The client in this case was smarter than his lawyer.

Footsteps and Last-Minute Agreements

The go-to-hell point is frequently a moving target (see chapter 7, "Positional Negotiation"). Earlier in this book, I referred to the "footsteps of the jury" syndrome (see chapter 1, "*Getting to YES*: Traditional Theory"). Prior to becoming a divorce lawyer, I served as an assistant district attorney for seven years, four and a half years of that as a felony trial lawyer. For felony prosecutions, I rarely engaged in any extensive plea bargaining—and sometimes none at all. Yet, I was continually amazed at how frequently the defendant would change his mind at the last moment and accept a nominal plea agreement or, occasionally, just plead guilty without any agreement. This would sometimes occur with the jury physically in the hallway, or even in the box. Once, in fact, in a major case, it occurred after my opening statement when the defendant was impressed with what the state intended to prove.

Although I would like to flatter myself and attribute some of those late-minute pleas to my reputation as a trial lawyer, the reality is that it had little to do with me personally but rather with the recognition that trial was at hand. Judges have footsteps, too, and knowing that the Day of Judgment is nigh can be very effective at causing a client to realistically focus on negotiating his own outcome.

Judicial Roadblock

Particularly in this field, there are courts that make it difficult (and sometimes impossible) to actually pick a firm go-to-hell trial date. You can be frustrated as all get out: "Why did he ever become judge anyway if he doesn't want to hear trials? Because he thinks he looks good in a black robe?" Still, some judges discourage divorce trials, and I've even known a few who absolutely refuse to hear them.

If you are on the side that cares less about the finality of the case (and usually there is one side that is less anxious than the other), you can actually take advantage of this unprofessional attitude by holding out for a better deal. Whichever side you are on, you need to know if the particular judge involved will, in fact, do his job in promoting finality. Therefore, research on the individual judge is critical.

Minting Negotiable Currency

In any event, planning for endstage negotiations is essential, and this planning needs to include face-saving for the other side. It gives your client no advantage if the eventual agreement is a great one on paper but the paper is not negotiable currency. Reaching an agreement for which enforcement mechanisms, no matter how persuasive, will have to be utilized is not the goal.

Money to Warm Cold Feet

Ideally (and few, if any, negotiations are ideal), at least one or more minor concessions should be held back for closure. In settlement parlance, it's called "leaving money on the table." Of course, in cases with limited resources or issues (which is most cases), this is not possible as there is little money to be left on the table (or in your client's pocket). However, if you have a case that is more involved, try not to give away the last dollar, especially if the other side seems less committed to the settlement. Save something for closing the deal at the last minute if the other side gets cold feet.

In his book *A Civil Action*, Jonathan Harr explained how the main character, attorney Jan Schlictmann, would hold settlement negotiations for a major case in a neutral location. In the corner would be a bottle of high-quality champagne, to be opened only in the event of a settlement. According to Schlictmann, the knowledge that the champagne was there sometimes helped the parties bridge the final gap.[1]

---

1. JONATHAN HARR, A CIVIL ACTION (1996).

A Few Strains of "Kumbaya"

Few of the successful negotiations in which I have been involved have concluded with everyone joining hands and singing "Kumbaya." Rather, most negotiating sessions end with both sides feeling stressed and wrung out and that they made too many (and sometimes all) of the concessions—conditions that are not in the least conducive to a celebration of any sort. Not infrequently, the second-guessing starts soon after the negotiations end—and sometimes before.

To address this situation, two processes are recommended.

First, if negotiations were separate, either due to caucus mediation or because they were not done in person, a summary of the agreement should be prepared immediately. If the negotiations were in person, the summary should be drafted in person. In the olden days (in which many lawyers still live), this would be done by dictating a settlement memorandum to a secretary. Today, a word-processing device can be used.

Second, the lawyers should meet individually with their clients and reaffirm the wisdom of reaching an agreement. In order to reach an agreement, the clients made compromises, meaning that they gave up something that they wanted. In addition, no settlement is ever perfect. In reality, the wisdom (or lack thereof) of any agreement is never apparent until sufficient time has expired to verify (or not!) its effects. In many cases, a party can dissipate the good aspects of an agreement or mitigate the bad parts. The lawyer needs to discourage the former and encourage the latter. This should start as soon as possible after negotiations have concluded—preferably immediately.

A longtime family law attorney from Louisiana, the late Arnold Gibbs, once told me about the concept of a "lagniappe." In Cajun country, where he grew up, a lagniappe was a small gift, perhaps a piece of candy, that he would receive from a store owner after his parents' purchase was complete. No additional cost and no reciprocation was requested or suggested. It was merely a throw-in, done to show appreciation for his parents' business. There is a danger in giving a lagniappe in a divorce settlement. The other side could feel that it did not ask for enough or that the deal was simply too favorable for the opposing side. Like all concepts, you have to be careful when and how to apply it. My Cajun friend, though, used it in certain circumstances after the negotiations were final; and you, too, could throw in a small, usually symbolic, additional benefit at the end without changing the settlement.

Summary

There are many strategies for planning for the endgame, and which strategy you employ will depend on the circumstances of the individual case. What is important is that you do, in fact, plan for the endgame and what you may need to do to bring the negotiations to a successful conclusion.

Becoming a Better Negotiator 22

Among the anomalies involved in the practice of law is the disparity between the substance of continuing legal education (CLE) programs and the reality of practice. As a rough, totally unscientific estimate, 90 percent of CLE programs in family law involve, in one sense or another, litigation skills. However, my surveys of family law attorneys across the country reveal that 90 percent—or more—of family law cases are resolved through negotiations. If you accept these estimates (or anywhere near them), that means that 90 percent of CLE deals with what lawyers actually do only 10 percent of their time.

Why is this so? Perhaps one reason is that litigation CLE is "sexier." Conducting cross-examination, making closing arguments, and presenting testimony are all skills shown on TV; and such shows do not aim to bore viewers. Trials are exciting. Settlement negotiations are not. Perhaps ego plays a role. (What? Divorce lawyers have egos? No way!) Machismo in law is trying cases, not settling them. Indeed, some lawyers think that even discussing settlement (see "Preparing the Client for Settlement") is a sign of weakness.

There may be other possibilities, but I believe that the answer is "none of the above." Rather, I suspect that most lawyers believe that litigation requires special skills entailing rigorous training, while settlement is intuitive and comparatively easy, i.e., that settlement merely requires taking a position and making compromises. This is true, but only in the same way that one might believe trial law is easy because it merely requires asking questions and making an argument.

Being a *good* trial lawyer requires skills and experience. The same applies to being a *good* negotiator, rather than just being a lawyer who negotiates. The difference in negotiations is more profound, however. Not only do the enhanced skills afford the client a better financial result, but, done skillfully, negotiating can enhance the opportunity for a more peaceful relationship with the ex-spouse in the future. Not only are these aims not contradictory, they are complementary. The less friction between the parties, the greater the incentive to cooperate in the future, not only in terms of parenting but financially as well.

So, if negotiating is not solely intuitive, what can you do to become a better negotiator? Below are a few suggestions on the topic.

Read This Book

Oh, wait, you are already doing that!

Read Other Material

There is a huge amount of material on the art of negotiations, ranging from philosophical to practical to intellectual. A starting point surely is Roger Fisher and William Ury's classic book *Getting to YES: Negotiating Agreement Without Giving In*.[1] In addition, there are substantial resources on how to negotiate in numerous different forums, many of which can be adopted for family law cases.

Reading books in other disciplines can also aid in becoming a better negotiator. As discussed throughout this book, negotiations involve an understanding of human beings and human emotions. Therefore, any book (or course) on psychology could be an invaluable

---

1. Roger Fisher & William Ury, Getting to YES: Negotiating Agreement Without Giving In (1981).

aid to settlement. A recent best seller, *Freakonomics*,[2] and its sequel, *SuperFreakonomics*,[3] for example, marry economic theory and pop psychology in areas as diverse as drug dealing and sumo wrestling. Of course, much of economic theory is premised on understanding human motivation, so study in that area could also find application to settlement negotiations. Furthermore, in settlement negotiations we are trying to sell our proposal. In addition to understanding psychology, books on marketing and sales could provide useful ideas on the art of persuasion.

Watch Other Lawyers

Prior to joining my present firm, my only experience in settlement negotiations was plea bargaining as a prosecutor (law schools in my day did not offer courses in alternative dispute resolution). Of course, plea bargaining is radically different from divorce settlement negotiations. Since the prosecutor has far less to lose at trial, the stakes are not the same on both sides of the table; and the settlement dynamics are far different from a divorce where both parties have skin in the game.

However, I had the privilege of watching Leonard Loeb, my boss and later my partner, negotiate divorce cases. Atlhough some of his style does not fit my personality, I learned and adopted a great deal of his technique.

For example, I saw one session in which Leonard was representing a wife in a long-term marriage whose wealthy husband had been caught philandering. Leonard opened the negotiating session as follows:

> *When I asked my client what she truly wanted arising from this divorce, she assured me that she really didn't care about property division or support. What she really wanted was to use a rusty razor and make him eligible for membership in the Vienna Boys Choir. Now, I assured her that the goal was not attainable in a literal sense, so I've had her translate it to dollars.*

---

[2]. Steven D. Levitt & Stephen J. Dubner, Freakonomics: A Rogue Economist Explores the Hidden Side of Everything (2005).
[3]. Steven D. Levitt & Stephen J. Dubner, Super Freakonomics: Global Cooling, Patriotic Prostitutes, and Why Suicide Bombers Should Buy Life Insurance (2009).

Although there is no way that I could ever make such an "opening statement" and keep a straight face, watching his style—and the reaction of the other lawyer—was highly instructive.

Of course, most lawyers are not so lucky: negotiations are not public sessions. Still, if you are an associate with an experienced partner, she may welcome a "second chair" in negotiations; and you can watch the styles of two lawyers in one setting.

Remember, though, that a negotiating style must fit your individual personality. Just like all recipes say "season to taste," all negotiating styles must be "seasoned" to fit the individual style of a particular attorney.

Take Courses in Negotiating

Just because you have been negotiating for years doesn't mean you can't do it better. Although, as stated above, there are far more legal education courses offered on litigation, there are, fortunately, quite a few on the skills of negotiating. Some of these skills can be found in mediation courses. Others can be found in collaborative law training. Still others can be found in business schools. These skills can include listening, planning, problem solving, and communicating.

Take Courses in Related Skills

Negotiating well requires a large set of skills, not all of which are taught in courses on negotiations. Courses in psychology, physiology, human development, marketing, and conflict negotiations all have skill sets that can be highly useful in negotiation sessions. After all, the goal of negotiating is to reach an agreement with other human beings. Therefore, understanding human relationships (psychology) and how humans listen and process information (physiology) and resolve conflicts would be highly helpful in this arena.

Mediation courses can be very helpful as well. Although mediation is not identical to settlement, many of the skills and techniques are transferable. Moreover, mediation is becoming more and more common as a standard settlement model in every divorce case. Even if you don't intend on becoming a mediator yourself, learning how a mediator is trained may be useful when representing a client in mediation.

In an ideal world, there would be a required course in law school simply on listening skills. Listening is not intuitive. Some people are better at it than others. Those who can listen well will pick up cues that can lead to far better negotiating skills. For those who are not intuitively good listeners, there are skills that you can learn that can make you better. For starters, read *The Family Lawyer's Guide to Building Successful Client Relationships* by Sanford M. Portnoy.[4] And as that great philosopher, Yogi Berra, once said, "You can observe a lot by just watching."[5]

Be Self-Critical

I heard a story once about a professional speaker. He said that when he gives a speech, there are three versions. There is the one that he plans to give. There is the one that he actually delivers when he improves on the original version while actually giving the speech. And "[i]f you want to hear a truly great speech," he said, "drive home with me afterward and hear the speech that I should have given."

Each of us can improve our skills by considering what we did right and wrong during an actual case. Do a self-analysis after each case. Ask yourself what you could have done better. Make every case a learning experience.

Get Feedback from Other Attorneys

Many times, our egos prevent us from asking for assistance. However, especially if you are a young lawyer, there is a great deal of experience available from lawyers who have been doing this for a long time. And many of these experienced lawyers would be pleased—even flattered— to share feedback. So, after completing an action (during the case is probably not wise), take an older lawyer to lunch or coffee. No CLE credit will be given, but it may be the best education you will ever get.

---

4. SANFORD M. PORTNOY, THE FAMILY LAWYER'S GUIDE TO BUILDING SUCCESSFUL CLIENT RELATIONSHIPS (ABA FAMILY LAW SECTION 2003).
5. BrainyQuote, Yogi Berra Quotes, http://www.brainyquote.com/quotes/quotes/y/yogiberra125285.html(last visited Oct. 13, 2012).

Get Feedback from Former Clients

Asking a former client for feedback may be helpful. Yes, there is a danger in this as you may hear things you don't want to hear. And there is a natural tendency to get defensive. But if you can park your ego at the door for a while, you may get a lot out of this exercise. It is, after all, the client whom you are serving.

In my firm, we do this in two different ways. First, we hold a post-judgement meeting (sort of like an autopsy) after every case. Often, we will not charge for that conference. It provides closure for the attorney-client relationship both personally and professionally and also an opportunity to ask for a critique.

There are clients who may not be comfortable providing such feedback in person, so we provide an anonymous opportunity. Approximately once a year, we mail an evaluation form that can be sent in anonymously. One of the nice side effects of this form is that the vast majority of former clients say only nice things—sometimes very nice things that make for pleasant reading. But although that is good for ego inflation, the education comes from the few who provide helpful criticisms and suggestions for improvement.

Be Creative

I am amazed at the number of times attorneys ask whether there is a form for a certain procedure. Many years ago, I taught a course for family law paralegals. After one class, a young lady shyly approached me and asked me whether a certain form was accurate. The form had been widely used throughout the state for many years, but, sure enough, there was an error. From then on, until the replacement form became commonplace, I would see lawyers robotically using the old form with the error.

On the other side of the coin, Minneapolis lawyer Stuart Webb did not like the concept of a lawyer as a combatant rather than as a problem solver. Believing that the threat of court was inimical to the future relationship between parents, he invented a form of law based on collaboration rather than adversity.[6] As discussed in this book (see chap-

---

6. Yishai Boyarin, *Generating Win-Win Results: Negotiating Conflicts in the Drafting Process of the Uniform Collaborative Law Act*, 38 Hofstra L. Rev. 495, 495 (2009).

ter 15, "Collaborative Divorce"), collaborative divorce is not the only negotiation method. However, it does illustrate what can happen when someone—forgive the cliché—thinks outside the box.

The point is this: Don't rely on forms. Don't believe that just because "that's the way it's always been done" means that "that's the only way to do it." Experiment. Learn. Then, please, share. Life is a learning process.

Summary

Life is a learning process. Although settling cases seems intuitive, there is a huge quantity of information available on the topic of becoming a better negotiator. Whether through reading material, courses, or personal efforts, all divorce lawyers should be making continuous efforts to improve their skills.

Index

A

Accessibility, of judge, 71–72
Agenda, for initial client meeting, 38–39
Anchoring, 126
Anger, 147
Annotation, for financial disclosure, 43
Arrogance, 144
Assessment, case, in planned early negotiation, 76–77
Assets
 big picture and, 21
 in buy-sell offer, 112
 listing of, 20
Assurance, providing, 32–33
Attorneys. *See* Lawyer(s)

B

Babbitt, Gerald, 55
Backward negotiating, 38–39, 144–145
Bargaining, positional
 advantages of, 45
 bracketing in, 46
 client understanding of, 38
 compromise and, 48–49
 go-to-hell point in, 47–48
 opening proposal in, 46–47
 optimal position in, 46
 positions in, 45–48
 principled negotiation and, 8
 ultimatum and, 48–49

BATNAs (Best Alternative To a Negotiated Agreement), 12–13, 39
Beautiful Mind, A (Nasar), 121
Beyond Reason: Using Emotions as You Negotiate (Fisher and Shapiro), 30
Big picture, 21–22
Books, for continuing education, 156–157
Bounds of Advocacy (American Academy of Matrimonial Lawyers), 130, 137
Boyarin, Yishai, 42, 96, 101
Bracketing, 38, 46
Bullying, 53
Buyout, support, 16–17
Buy-sell offer, 112

C

Children
　best interests of, 83
　conflict minimization and, 82–83
　in cooperative divorce, 105
　custody of, 81–83
　effects of divorce on, 82
　as family law–specific issue, 81–84
　placement *vs.* support of, 83–84
　visitation of, 81–83
Churchill, Winston, 36
Civil Action, A (Harr), 151
CLE. *See* Continuing legal education (CLE)
Client(s)
　in collaborative divorce, 100–101
　emotions (*See* Emotions)
　ethics of communication with, 136–137
　feedback from former, 160
　as final decision maker, 149–150
　intentions, material facts *vs.*, 130–131
　judge meeting with, 72–73
　meeting, 38–40 (*See also* Four-way meeting)
　motivations of, 117
　preparation, 35–37
　pro se opposing, 57–61
Closure, concessions for, 151, 152–153
Collaborative divorce
　agreement to proceed in, 97
　cooperative divorce *vs.*, 105
　costs of, 100
　decline in, 104
　defined, 95
　disqualification agreement in, 98, 99–100, 108
　domestic violence and, 99, 101
　downsides of, 99–101
　ethics and, 134–135
　financial advantages of, 134–135
　financial professional in, 98–99
　incompatibility of clients and lawyers with, 100–101
　judge in, 99
　litigation and, 96
　mental health professional in, 98
　mental illness and, 99
　as multidisciplinary process, 95–96
　overview of, 103–104

risks of, 99–100
screening in, 101
settlement rates in, 100
substance abuse and, 99
withdrawal agreement in, 96
Colorado Bar Association, 134
Communication
 ethics and, 136–137
 nonverbal, 26, 38
 problems, listening and, 9
Compensation, for planned early negotiation, 77–78
Compromise, ultimatum *vs.*, 48–49
Concessions, for closure, 151, 152–153
Conclusion, of four-way meeting, 67
Conflict, children and, 82–83
Continuing legal education (CLE), 155–161
Control
 of emotions, 29–34
 of negotiation timing, lack of, 25
Cookie cutter technique, 111–112
Cooperative divorce
 antagonism and, 105
 children and, 105
 collaborative divorce *vs.*, 105
 financial professional in, 106–107
 judge in, 107
 mediation and, 106
 mental health professional in, 106
 nonbinding nature of, 105
 overview of, 104–106
 reasons for, 107–108
 sample agreement form for, 109
 trial and, 107
 understandings necessary for, 105–106
Cordiality, 140–141
Costs
 of collaborative divorce, 100
 of litigation *vs.* settlement, 36–37
 of planned early negotiation, 77–78
Counsel. *See* Opposing counsel
Counseling, emotions and, 30
Court, in nontrial trial, 113
Creative settlement technique(s)
 buy-sell offer as, 112
 "cut the cookie" as, 111–112
 extra money and, 116
 friends in, 115
 joint recommendation as, 114–115
 kindness and, 118
 "nontrial trial" as, 113–114
 reasons for, 111
 "taking issue off the table" as, 116–118
Creativity, 160–161
Criteria, objective, 11–12
Crying, 32
Culture, negotiation and, 47
Custody, of children, 81–83

D

Deadlines, 141–142
Debts
 big picture and, 21
 listing of, 20

Disclaimer, for pro se opposing
    party, 58–59
Disclosure
    benefits of full voluntary, 41–43
    courts and, 42–43
    electronic, 43
    emotions and, 42
    fully annotated, 43
    importance of, 142–143
    methods, 43–44
    statements, financial,
        negotiation timing and, 16
    voluntary, 142–143
Discovery, negotiation timing
    and, 15–16, 25
Disqualification agreement, in
    collaborative divorce, 98,
    99–100, 108
Distrust, 36
Divorce
    collaborative (*See* Collaborative
        divorce)
    cooperative (*See* Cooperative
        divorce)
    effects of, on children, 82
    preponderance of settlement
        in, 1–2
    stages of proceedings in, 23–24
Domestic violence, collaborative
    divorce and, 99, 101
Doubt, client, 36
Dresher, Melvin, 125

E
Education
    continuing, 155–161
    lack of focus on settlement
        in, 2
    in negotiation, 158
    in negotiation-related skills,
        158–159
Electronic information,
    disclosure of, 43
Emotions
    advantages of, 30
    angry, 147
    atmosphere and, 26
    controlling, 29–34
    cooperative divorce and, 105
    counseling and, 30
    disadvantages of, 30
    disclosure and, 42
    fearful, 32–33, 48
    in four-way meeting, 66
    getting personal and, 146–147
    listening and, 31–32
    long-term strategy and, 33–34
    malpractice and, 24–25
    mediation and, 90
    negotiation timing and, 17,
        24, 26
    planned early negotiation
        and, 78
    professionalism and, 34
    questions and, 31
    respect and, 135–136
    separation of, from problem, 9
    validation of, 32
Ethics
    in client communication,
        136–137
    client intentions *vs.* material
        facts in, 130–131
    in collaborative divorce, 134–135
    family law and, 129
    issue mixing and, 137

of opposing counsel, 53–54
of position representation, 39
and respect of opposing side, 135–136
truthfulness and, 130–131
withdrawal and, 131–134
Experience, of mediator, 90–91

F
Face-saving
  negotiable currency and, 150–151
  support and, 86–87
Face-to-face negotiation, 17
Facilitative mediation, 91–92
Facts, material, client intentions *vs.*, 130–131
Family Law Section (FLS), of ABA, 1
Fear, 32–33, 48
Feedback
  from former clients, 160
  from other lawyers, 159
Feelings. *See* Emotions
Feibleman, Gilbert, 19, 31, 32
Financial disclosure statements
  annotated, 43
  benefits of full voluntary, 41–43
  importance of, 142–143
  negotiation timing and, 16
Financial professional
  in collaborative divorce, 98–99
  in cooperative divorce, 106–107
First offer, 19
First step, 143–144
Fisher, Roger, 7, 8, 9–10, 12, 30, 86, 156
Flood, Merrill, 125

Form, cooperative divorce agreement, 109
Four-way meeting
  conclusion of, 67
  emotions in, 66
  in family law, 63
  location of, 64–65
  as negotiation format, 18
  observing opposing party client/counsel interaction at, 26
  physical positioning in, 65
  preparation for, 65
  reasons for, 63–64
  recess in, 66
  setting tone of, 66
  timing of, 64
Freakonomics (Levitt and Dubner), 157
Friend
  involving, as creative settlement technique, 115
  opposing counsel as, 54–56

G
Gain, options for mutual, 10–11
GAL. *See* Guardian ad litem (GAL)
Games of complete information, 122
Game theory, 121–128
  anchoring in, 126
  background of, 121–122
  nonzero sum games in, 127
  prisoner's dilemma in, 125–126
  Texas Hold 'Em in, 124–125
  ultimatum game in, 123

Game theory (*continued*)
  utilization of, 127–128
  zero sum games in, 127
Gandhi, Mohandas K., 5
Getting to YES: Negotiating Agreement Without Giving In (Fisher and Ury), 7, 86, 156
Gibbs, Arnold, 152
Goals, establishment of reasonable, 40
Go-to-hell point, 47–48
Grief, stages of, 24
Guardian ad litem (GAL), 82

H
Harr, Jonathan, 151
Harris, Sondra, 61
Hearings, negotiation timing and, 16
Herman, Gregg, 95
Human development, 158

I
Incentive, work, support and, 85–86
Income creation, support payments and, 2–3
Insecurity, 144
Intentions, material facts *vs.* client, 130–131
Interests
  of children, 83
  positions *vs.*, 10
  shared, 11
Intimidation
  by judge, 70
  by opposing counsel, 52–53

J
Joint recommendation, 114–115
Joy of Settlement, The (ABA Family Law Section), 1, 3, 20, 143
Judge
  accessibility of, 71–72
  client meeting by, 72–73
  in collaborative divorce, 99
  in cooperative divorce, 107
  intimidation by, 70
  in lawyer preparation, 37
  leadership of, 70
  management by, 71
  as mediator, 92
  in nontrial trial, 113–114
  pretrial and, 72
  role of, 69–73
  settlement facilitation by, 70–72
Judicial roadblock, 150–151

K
Kapp, C. Terrence, 20, 21
Kindness, 118
Kübler-Ross, Elisabeth, 24

L
Lagniappe, 152–153
Lande, John, 75, 77–78, 101
Last-minute agreements, 150
Lawyer(s)
  as continuing education resource, 157–158
  feedback from other, 159
  opposing counsel
    "book" on, 51–52
    competitive, 54

cooperative, 54
ethics of, 53–54
as friend, 54–56
intimidating, 52–53
knowing, 52
negotiating with, 51–56
opening meeting with, 52
pro se, 57–61
rapport with, 52
respect for, 135–136, 140–141
untrustworthy, 53–54
Lawyering with Planned Early Negotiation: How You Can Get Good Results for Clients and Make Money (Lande), 75–76
Leadership, of judge, 70
Legal education, lack of focus on settlement in, 2
Listening
  emotions and, 31–32
  importance of, 9
  respect and, 136
  response planning *vs.*, 9–10
  summarization and, 31
Litigation
  collaborative divorce and, 96
  cost of, 36–37
  focus on, in legal education, 2
  settlement *vs.*, 3, 36–37
Little picture, 21–22
Location, for four-way meeting, 64–65
Loeb, Leonard, 2, 87, 157
Long-term, emotions and, 33–34
Lying, 130

M
Mail, negotiation by, 17
Malpractice, emotions and, 24–25
Management, by judges, 71
Marketing, 158
Mediation
  cooperative divorce and, 106
  courses, 158
  emotions and, 90
  facilitative, 91–92
  increasing use of, 89
  judges as mediator in, 92
  lawyers as mediators in, 92
  limited skill and experience of mediator in, 90–91
  mediator types in, 92–93
  mental health professionals as mediators in, 92
  pitfalls of, 90–92
  postsettlement in, 94
  power disparity in, 91
  preparation for, 93–94
  reasons for success of, 89–90
  selection of mediator in, 92–93
  social workers as mediators in, 9, 92
  unrepresented parties in, 91
Meeting, client, 38–40. *See also* Four-way meeting
Mental health professional
  in collaborative divorce, 98
  in cooperative divorce, 106
  as mediator, 92
Mental illness
  collaborative divorce and, 99
  pro se representation and, 60
Mixing, of issues, 116–117, 137

Mock trial, 114
Model Code of Professional Responsibility, 3
Model Rules of Professional Conduct (ABA), 129, 130, 131–132, 134
Motivations, client, 117
Mutual gain, 10–11

N
Nasar, Sylvia, 121
Nash, John, 121, 122, 127
Negotiation
  backward, 38–39, 144–145
  convincing client to take up, 35–37
  courses in, 158
  four-way meeting format for, 18, 26
  importance of, 2
  by mail, 17
  methods, 17–18
  with opposing counsel, 51–56
  order of, 20–21
  planned early (*See* Planned early negotiation (PEN))
  principled, 7–12
  refusal of, 145–146
  by telephone, 17
  timing of, 15–17
  transparent, 49
  two-sided face-to-face, 17
Nichol, Chic, 9
Nichol, Mimi, 9
Nontrial trial, 113–114
Nonverbal communication, 26, 38
Nonzero sum games, 127

O
Objectivity, 11–12
Offer, first, 19
Opening proposal, in positional negotiation, 46–47
Opposing counsel
  "book" on, 51–52
  competitive, 54
  cooperative, 54
  ethics of, 53–54
  as friend, 54–56
  intimidating, 52–53
  knowing, 52
  negotiating with, 51–56
  opening meeting with, 52
  pro se, 57–61
  rapport with, 52
  respect for, 135–136, 140–141
  untrustworthy, 53–54
Optimal position, 46
Options, for mutual gain, 10–11
Order of negotiation, 20–21

P
Patience, 26
PEN. *See* Planned early negotiation (PEN)
People, separation of problem and, 8–10
Perception, 12–13
Personal, avoiding the, 146–147
Physiology, 158
Placement, child support *vs.*, 83–84
Planned early negotiation (PEN)
  advantages of, 78
  case assessment in, 76–77

compensation for, 77–78
disadvantages of, 78
emotions and, 78
escape hatch for, 77
fear of, 76–78
information exchange in, 77
principles of, 75–76
Poker, 124–125, 127
Politeness, 140–141
Position(s)
  interests *vs.*, 10
  optimal, 46
  in positional negotiation, 45–48
Positional bargaining. *See* Bargaining, positional
Postsettlement, in mediation, 94
Power disparity, mediation and, 91
Preparation
  client, 35–37
  for four-way meeting, 65
  importance of, 147–148
  lawyer, 37–38
  for mediation, 93–94
Pretrials, 72, 113
Principled negotiation, 7–12
Prisoner's dilemma, 125–126
Problem, separation of people and, 8–10
Proceedings, stages of divorce, 23–24
Professionalism, emotions and, 34
Pro se party
  categories of, 58
  disclaimers with, 58–59
  impoverished, 58–59
  as mentally ill, 60
  negotiation strategies with, 57–60
  as penny pincher, 59
  as professional lawyer, 59
  as pure evil, 59–60
  risks with, 60–61
Psychology, 156–157, 158. *See also* Game theory

Q
Questions, emotions and, 31

R
Rabin, Yitzhak, 36
Rapport, with opposing counsel, 52
Recess, in four-way meeting, 66
Refusal to negotiate, 145–146
Respect, for opposing side, 135–136, 140–141
Response planning, listening *vs.*, 9–10
Rounding, of figures, 20

S
Saucy, Paul, 19, 32
Schlictmann, Jan, 151
Screening, in collaborative divorce, 101
Self-criticism, 159
Separation, of people and problem, 8–10
Settlement
  cost of, 36–37
  lack of focus on, in legal education, 2
  litigation *vs.*, 3, 36–37

Settlement (*continued*)
  preponderance of, in divorce, 1–2
  as weakness, 37
Shapiro, Daniel, 30
Sheedy, Patrick, 63
"Shirking," 85–86
Simplification, of negotiations, 20
Skill, of mediator, 90–91
Social workers, as mediators, 9, 92
Spangler, Brad, 12
Stages
  of divorce proceedings, 23–24
  of grief, 24
Stubbornness, 144
Substance abuse, collaborative divorce and, 99
Sullivan, Mark, 143
Summarization
  listening and, 31
  of settlement agreement, 152
Sunsets, 141–142
Support
  buyout, 16–17
  face-saving and, 86–87
  incentive to work and, 85–86
  income creation and, 2–3
  placement *vs.*, 83–84
  "shirking" and, 85–86

T
Table, round, 18–19
Taking issue off the table, 116–118
Telephone negotiation, 17
Tesler, Pauline, 96
Texas Hold 'Em, 124–125
Thaler, Richard, 126
Timing
  of first step, 143–144
  of four-way meeting, 64
  of negotiation, 15–17
    after trial, 16–17
    discovery and, 15–16, 25
    emotions and, 17, 24, 26
    financial disclosure statements and, 16
    hearings and, 16
    importance of, 24–25
    issues in, 25–26
    lack of control over, 25
    order of negotiation and, 20–21
    planned early, 78
    recognition of proper, 26
    on trial day, 16
  of withdrawal, 132–133
Transparent negotiation, 49
Trial
  cooperative divorce and, 107
  fear of, 150
  go-to-hell point and, 48
  mock, 114
  negotiation after, 16–17
  negotiation on day of, 16
  nontrial, 113–114
  roadblocks to, 150–151
Trust, 36, 53–54
Truthfulness, ethics and, 130–131
Tucker, Albert W., 125
Twenty-four-hour rule, 34
Two-sided face-to-face negotiation, 17

U

Ultimatum(s)
   compromise *vs.*, 48–49
   in game theory, 123
   not giving, 141
Uniform Collaborative Law
      Act, 101
Ury, William, 7, 8, 9–10, 12, 86, 156

V

Validation, of emotions, 32
Vietnam War, 18
Violence, domestic, collaborative divorce and, 99, 101
Visitation, of children, 81–83

W

Walk-away point, 39
Wallerstein, Judith, 82
Weakness, settlement as, 37
Withdrawal
   ABA on, 131–132
   ethics and, 131–134
   noisy, 133
   normal, 133–134
   process of, 133–134
   timing of, 132–133
Work incentive, support and, 85–86

Z

Zero sum games, 127